Technology and Growth

Technology and Growth

The Price We Pay

E. J. Mishan

PRAEGER PUBLISHERS
New York · Washington

BOOKS THAT MATTER

Published in the United States of America in 1970
by Pràeger Publishers, Inc.
111 Fourth Avenue, New York, N.Y. 10003

Second printing, 1971

Library of Congress Catalog Card Number: 70-105282

Originally published in Great Britain
as GROWTH: *The Price We Pay* by Staples Press in 1969

Printed in the United States of America

Contents

Part VI: Conclusion and Appendices

Preface

It is unnecessary to remark that my convictions about the ends of
economic policy do not accord with popular preconceptions. But
neither do I imagine that I am quite alone in this respect. The skilled
economist immersed for the greater part of the day in pages of formulae
and statistics does occasionally feel a twinge of doubt about the relevance of his contribution to the welfare of society. True, there is at the
tip of his mind some faltering image of the blessings heaped on mankind as a result of rapid economic growth – a growing assortment of
automobiles, television sets, vacuum cleaners, refrigerators, washing
machines, electric tooth brushes and other anti-drudge devices, also
increased education, increased air travel, antibiotics, pesticides, and
reduced infantile mortality. And yet, glancing at the irresistible spread
of steel and concrete, at the plague of motorized traffic, at the growing
impatience and tenseness of people, his thoughts may catch at a deeper
apprehension of reality. For a moment, perhaps, he will dare to wonder
whether it is really worth it; whether economic progress over the last
couple of centuries has succeeded only in making life increasingly
complex, frantic and wearing. The speed of travel grows from year to
year, and from year to year more time is devoted in moving from one
place to another. Physically, however, we are more idle and our lives
more sedentary than our fathers. We know the world's business from
minute to minute, and practically nothing of the people who live in our
neighbourhood. Far removed from the forces of nature, denizens of the
new subtopia, we are degenerating into a breed of passenger-spectators
whose first impulse on awakening is to reach for a switch.

Like the rest of us, however, the economist must keep moving, and
since such misgivings about the over-all value of economic growth
cannot be formalized or numerically expressed, they are not permitted
seriously to modify his practical recommendations. To be sure, various
aspects of the social order are under continual attack by writers and
intellectuals. But such attacks are expected in the normal course of
events and, since such writers seldom have any claim to special economic knowledge, their strictures and dire predictions do not disturb

the public unduly. Indeed the public has a remarkable faith in the ultimate beneficence of industrial progress, a faith which, it seems to think, could, in the last resort, be redeemed by modern economics. For this reason, a critique of economic growth by an economist may be taken more seriously. And certainly something will be gained if the public learns to appreciate the closeness of the links between rapid economic development and many of the unpleasanter features of our civilization. Once this is accomplished, the way is open to a general realization that there are more fundamental issues than just 'forward' or 'back'; that there are critical social choices yet to be debated if we can but turn our ears from the daily chanting of efficiency slogans reminiscent of 'Four legs good: two legs bad'.

II

This volume is offered to the public as a more popular version of *The Costs of Economic Growth*[1] which first appeared in April 1967. Though originally intended for the educated layman, in the process of writing it I had too sensitive an eye to its future reception by my colleagues. The consequence of anticipating possible objections from economists has inevitably had the effect of making the book, at least in the earlier parts, less readable to non-economists. Though intelligible, these parts cannot be read without close attention and perhaps study, and this has acted to prevent the original work from being easily accessible to the wider public I had hoped to reach.

In abridging and simplifying some parts of the argument, and in deleting altogether some of the more arid passages (believed necessary to placate the more fastidious professionals) I have taken a particular care not to dilute the content of my main contentions. Indeed, I have taken the opportunity to reinforce them in a number of places by more exact wording and by the inclusion of additional material.

III

The contents of this volume are arranged in five parts (ignoring the appendices and concluding remarks in Part VI). The first part contains a criticism of popular attitudes towards economic matters and the way

[1] Published by Staples Press, London, and by Praeger, New York.

in which such popular attitudes, passing for economic sagacity, impose severe political limitations on the opportunities facing a wealthy country such as Britain. Part II begins by introducing the reader to the notion of 'spillover effects' as the most potent cause of public disamenity in the post-war period. The later three chapters outline simple proposals for their future containment. Part III illustrates the devastation wreaked on our environment since the war by reference to those 'spillover effects' associated with urban development, mass migration, tourism, and motorized traffic.

A market economy adjusted so as to overcome all 'spillover effects' would be an immense improvement over the existing uncorrected system. But it is not a panacea. There could still be no assurance that the more discriminating economic growth resulting from the adjustment would tend to promote the general welfare. Part IV, therefore, goes on to disclose other grave shortcomings in the existing market-actuated choice mechanism. Here again, however, enlightened legislation could go far to remedy such shortcomings – so further extending to the citizen the area of significant choice. In contrast, the disturbing implications of economic growth considered in Part V – which do not appear to lend themselves to formal analysis but which form an essential part of the agenda in any inquiry concerning the welfare value of economic growth – seem to be inseverably linked with technological progress.

IV

As I shall remind the reader in the Foreword and in the Concluding Chapter, no attempt has been made in this volume to present a balanced picture of social gains and losses arising from economic development in wealthy communities. I am concerned to reveal only some of the important connections between economic development and social welfare, chiefly those that are imperfectly understood and frequently overlooked by the citizen. I have no inhibitions either about divulging my sense of dismay at what is happening to our civilization since the book is not offered as a work of scholarship but rather as a tract for the times.

This limited objective serves to explain another apparent deficiency, the impressive lack of documentation. There are almost no references to the professional journal literature, nor indeed to the more popular works on political economy ranging from Adam Smith's *Wealth of Nations* to postwar monographs such as Hayel's *Road to Serfdom* and Friedman's *Capitalism and Freedom*. In particular, in Part V, there are no references to many extremely relevant passages of Plato and to Sir Karl Popper's critique thereof in his *Open Society and Its Enemies*. In what I hope to be a popular essay in persuasion I wish to avoid any dissipation of the force of my arguments by scattering the pages with learned comments pointing to similarities and differences between my views and those of more celebrated authors. As for documentation of current instances of excessive social costs, in an exposition of principles the examples are chosen largely for the light they shed on the principles. And though it would have been possible to draw on some of the recent studies to illustrate the magnitudes of some limited 'spillover effects', such as river effluence, I attach far greater importance to promoting a public awareness of their nature and of the ways they ought to enter economic calculation.

Finally, some readers may complain of a lack of detailed proposals or, worse, a lack of politically practicable proposals. But, at a time when the decencies of civilized living are daily beset by the exigencies of rapid material development, detailed proposals are secondary to what I deem to be the main task; that of convincing people of the need of radical change in our habitual ways of looking at economic events. As for political practicability, it is not too hard to foster a reputation for sound judgement and realism by a conspicuous display of moderation in moving with the times and a care to suggest nothing that the public is not just about ready to accept in any case. Such political sense has its uses, but it has nothing to contribute in any radical reassessment of social policy. Ideas that seem, at first, to be doomed to political impotence may strike root in the imagination of ordinary men and women, spreading and growing in strength until ready to emerge in political form. For what is politically feasible depends, in the last resort, on the active influences on public opinion.

v

I am indebted to the gentle persistence of Mrs Miriam Klipper for finally convincing me that there are significant differences between an intelligible prose style and a popular one. It remains to be seen whether

I have the capacity to benefit from her repeated advice and exhortation. I wish also to reproduce the acknowledgements made in the original work; to acknowledge the courtesy of the editors of *The Journal of Transport Economics and Policy* for permission to reprint as Appendix C a less technical version of my original Note in the May 1967 issue of that Journal. I must also acknowledge the courtesy of the editor of *British Industry*, Mr B. R. Russell, for his immediate response to my request to borrow some material from an article of mine that appeared in the March 1964 issue. Professor John Spraos of University College, London, was kind enough to read through the first draft of the Appendix A on the balance of payments. I am indebted to him for drawing my attention to some loose ends in the arguments and for making suggestions that substantially improved the presentation. The generosity of three of my colleagues at the London School of Economics in permitting me to inflict on them various parts of the unfinished manuscript during a period when the work of the School was making heavy demands on them is most gratefully recorded. Mr Laurence Harris and Dr Lionel Needleman both gave freely of their time in discussing with me a variety of issues that arose in connection with my first draft of Part V. Each of them pointed out blemishes in the original formulation. Dr Needleman, in addition to uncovering a number of stylistic infelicities, persuaded me to revise certain passages to distinct advantage. Mr Kurt Klappholz, with whom over the last ten years I have enjoyed countless discussions on problems concerning the relation between social welfare and economic policy, offered to read through the whole of the first draft, chapter by chapter. In the process of advising me at every turn in the arguments, he drew my attention to a host of defects in the arrangement and exposition. Though each of my colleagues is in broad sympathy with my views, I would not wish to implicate any of them in the details of my thesis, nor in the remaining defects for which I alone am responsible.

E. J. M.

Foreword

Contrary to their fashionable phrases about the need to face change, those who proclaim themselves to be in the vanguard of new thought prove to be in the iron clutch of economic dogma, much of it provided by famous economists of the past as a guide to policy in a world different from our own. Free trade, free competition, sustained economic growth, the free movement of peoples – these were, for Britain and America, at least the dominant economic aspirations of the nineteenth century. Nor were they entirely irrelevant after the turn of the century. Indeed, one might subscribe to such doctrines without self-deception until the close of World War II. For it was only after the first phase of the post-war recovery in Europe that one could descry the shape of things to come and, in that vision, doubt the relevance of these once-emancipating liberal doctrines to the momentous developments being wrought on our lives by the increasing pace of science and technology. The more salient among these developments are (1) the unprecedented expansion of the human species having ecological consequences we are only beginning to perceive, (2) the growing speed of technological advance and, as a corollary, the growing speed of obsolescence of skills, of knowledge and of culture, both esoteric and popular, and (3) the post-war surge of affluence in the West, much of it channelled into communications, in particular the mushroom growth of television, automobile ownership, air travel and mass tourism, phenomena that over a few short years have created a complex of urgent problems. Although the suddenness of these developments has caught us off our guard one might have thought that a modest concern with the welfare of society would have suggested the wisdom of setting aside inherited dogma and challenged us to think about what is taking place around us.

There may well be good explanations why this has not yet happened. It is possible that our forms of government are better adapted to a more leisurely age, one in which social grievances could be redressed and problems met as they arose. Significant events, one felt assured, took time to shape themselves. Institutions need only change through the slow accumulation of knowledge and experience. As for the physical environment about us, it could be depended upon to hold its form for many years together. Thus men conditioned themselves to detect in the passage of events familiar patterns and parallels, and lulled their apprehensions whenever catastrophe appeared imminent with aphorisms about the illusion of change and about the basic sameness of the world in spite of appearances to the contrary.

Moreover, no provision is made, nor perhaps could it be made, for the sort of training that might fit a man to think about and judge of the effects on the welfare of ordinary people of a gathering eruption of science and technology in pressure sufficient to splinter the framework of our institutions and to sunder the moral foundations on which they have been raised. In the course of his work a person of trained intelligence has little incentive to turn his mind to such tremendous questions. Whether working in the physical or the social sciences, those scholars who are not struggling abreast of the cumulating literature in their chosen field are struggling for recognition chiefly by attempting to publish original scientific work – an aim that is facilitated not by broadening but by narrowing yet further the focus of their inquiries. Economists are not excepted. Although many are interested in more than mathematical refinement and generalization for its own elegant sake, they do not tend to wonder aloud whether, for instance, the last two decades of material growth in the West has, on balance, further promoted the happiness of mankind. Such speculation, they might suppose, is better relegated to the amateur debating society. The world has more important matters to attend to. Such broad questions cannot, in any case, be systematically discussed using the purely technical apparatus of the social sciences; nor can they be discussed without the frequent invocation of 'value judgements'. And any social scientist who will dare to go so far in offending against custom and usage must be prepared to bear the withering scorn of those of the fraternity who have been more zealous in safeguarding their methodological chastity.

II

Whatever the explanation, we live in paradoxical circumstances. Notwithstanding the fact that bringing the Jerusalem of economic growth to 'England's green and pleasant land' has so far conspicuously reduced both the greenness and the pleasantness, economic growth remains the most respectable catchword in the current political vocabulary. Even the younger men of today, struggling for the reins of power, habitually disregard, in their diagnoses of the times, the new sources of social conflict and social discontent emerging around us. They continue to give expression to the basic doctrines of their fathers and spin rhetoric out of the growth theme in blithe unconcern of the spreading jungle of problems stemming directly from the material prosperity of the last decade or so. They persist in minting phrases combining 'new' and 'change' and 'modern' and 'dynamic' as though these were cardinal virtues and in effect offer us all salvation by science – and via more exports.

One factor that enables them to get away with their routine push-and-shove exhortation to the public is the post-war 'discovery' of that latest addition to the armoury of the Establishment, the economic index. A remarkably simple thing in itself, a mere number in fact, yet one that is treated with unabashed reverence. Apparently one has but to consult it to comprehend the entire condition of society. Among the faithful, and they are legion, any doubt that, say, a four per cent growth rate, as revealed by the index, is better for the nation than a three per cent growth rate is near-heresy; is tantamount to a doubt that four is greater than three. Such a doubt is not much worse than the doubt that economic growth itself, like the growth of knowledge, is not 'on balance' a good thing. None the less, since many of the influences on our well-being (and possibly the major influences) – and in this essay we are to be concerned wholly with well-being, with welfare, satisfaction or happiness; possibly not measurable but certainly meaningful – do not lend themselves easily to the number system, it is not hard to show, as I propose to do in the following chapters, that doubts about a positive connection between social welfare and the index of economic growth are amply justified.

Some of these influences, however, have not been lost on economists, though I shall suggest that the extent of their impact on social welfare has been grossly underestimated. Since the turn of the century they have been systematically treated under the heading of 'external economies and diseconomies' or, to use the more popular and suggestive jargon adopted in this volume, 'spillover effects'.

None the less, there are other criticisms that go beyond those that may be encompassed by spillover effects. These other criticisms, moreover, do not depend for their validity and force upon the particular institutions through which a liberal or communist society allocates its growing resources and distributes its products. The economic growth of an affluent society under the direction of a highly centralized planning commission would be no less vulnerable to such criticisms than would be a decentralized and free enterprise system.

III

What I wish to be concluded from this essay might usefully be summarized here: that the popular post-war dichotomy drawn between the 'establishment' on the one hand and the 'progressives' on the other – or, to vary the terminology, between the traditionalists and the old school on the one hand and the 'modernizers' and 'pacemakers' on the other – has served to confuse the chief issue that confronts us: that of seeking to adjust the environment to gratify man's nature or of adjusting man's nature to an environment determined predominantly by 'efficiency considerations', that is, by technological advance.

One could, of course, decide to use words differently and, therefore, to agree that the issue is that between 'facing change' and 'going on in the same old way', provided that we dissociate 'facing change' from the inertia of mere momentum and, more specifically, from the orthodox measures that invariably feature on the agenda of our would-be 'pace-setters' – more competition, more exports, increased efficiency and, above all of course, faster economic growth. For those who, from habit as much as conviction, hanker after these nostrums, who are impatient to hustle us into the future, painful though it be, are not, on an alternative use of language, facing the twentieth century at all. They are merely trimming their sails to the winds of orthodoxy.

The phrase, 'facing the twentieth century', should refer, instead, to the need, in the face of a new and incalculable power of modern technology, to surrender the simple faith in the ultimate beneficence of industrial progress guided only by ancient presumption in favour of liberal economic doctrines. Stated more positively, the younger generation will be facing the future with honesty only as it brings itself to face the strain of thinking through the consequences, tangible and intangible, of the current drift into the future and, in doing so, recognizes that in today's world the old liberal economic harmonies are not to be found; that enlightened self-interest does not always walk hand in hand with natural justice; that on many issues painful choices have to be made; and more crucial yet, that the needs of men and the needs of technology may prove to be irreconcilable.

I am far from being unaware that many of my arguments in the later chapters will not stand up to so-called scientific scrutiny; that many assertions are made without the attempt to present evidence. For this I hold the present state of knowledge to be at fault, not my arguments. Owing to the speed with which events have overtaken our analytic and statistical techniques we have not yet evolved methods for estimating the more outstanding spillover effects of the post-war era. Yet such is the perverse faith in figures, that what cannot be quantified is all too frequently left out of the calculations altogether. There is apparently a strong prejudice among research workers against admitting that the unmeasurable effects could be more significant than the measurable ones. In mans cases, therefore, conclusions reached on the basis of the measurable effects only are unwarranted.

Since there does not appear much likelihood of our being able to estimate many of these swiftly proliferating spillover effects in the near future, it is all the more urgent that they be brought to the public's attention in the most graphic manner rather than have the practice continue of relegating them to an apologetic footnote. The undeniable fact that no estimates have been made, or are likely to be made shortly, about the magnitude of some untoward social effect arising in the normal pursuit of commerce, need not intimidate the economist from occasionally respecting the plain and inescapable evidence of his own senses. Nor should such a fact inhibit his reasonable conjectures about future consequences if present trends remain unchecked.

IV

As for those consequences of rapid technological advance that do not, even in principle, lend themselves easily to measurement, one cannot await the advent of a more accommodating methodology before considering them in earnest since they seem yet more portentous than those which are at least measurable in principle. Here, the appeal to the reader must of necessity be in terms of familiar experience and intuitive knowledge. It should be clear that it would not have been possible to write Part V if I had continued to submit to the self-denying ordinance of the good economic theorist, that tastes be accepted as data and that people's choices are final. For pure economic analysis, whatever is the nature or the standards of society's observed wants (or whatever they are becoming under the impact of events, technological, commercial, or political), is a matter of complete indifference. Such an indifference need not – though alas it sometimes does – become a part of the convictions of the practising economist. Indeed, if one is seriously concerned with social welfare, the effects of existing economic systems on the standards of taste or, for that matter, on the very character of people, are of primary importance.

Of course, one may assert, in an outburst of magnificent detachment, that a fondness for *The Adventures of Superman* is to be respected no less than a fondness for Milton's *Paradise Lost*; that a preference for the strains of 'Tease me, do!' is not to be ranked below one for Beethoven's Choral. One may assert it, but in fact nobody believes it. And we do not act as if we believe it. We are hardly surprised to learn of a youth who once doted on *The Adventures of Superman* becoming disenchanted with that sort of fare and moving on towards an appreciation of and eventual enthusiasm for *Paradise Lost*. The reverse sequence would not be credible. We should be stupefied to learn of a lover of Shakespeare or Milton's poetry turning instead for fulfilment to *The Adventures of Superman* – unless it was also pointed out that he was entering his dotage. Similarly, we should be hard put to imagine a lover of Beethoven's music turning for more lasting satisfaction to such items as 'Tease me, do!' It may be inferred therefore that we do not believe that all tastes are of equal value.

Again, one may assert – especially when considering the possibility of some unfortunate development – that future generations might not mind living under conditions that are repellent to us; they will, after all, have become accustomed to them. This may well be a fact: one can easily visualize a Huxley's *Brave New World* of emotional cretins seeking above all a frictionless passage through life and combating any disturbance to their equanimity with a euphoric pill. But the relevant question is whether human adaptation to such conditions enhances the quality and experience of living or otherwise. That we tacitly reject this argument whenever it touches our immediate concerns is borne out by our response to any current abuse. Apparently no one thinks it fit to propose that an existing social evil be left unremedied until such time as people have become sufficiently dull or hardened or corrupt as no longer to care about it.

Without making an explicit statement on the essential ingredients of the good life I none the less argue in Part V as if such ingredients do exist. So that if it were true that people are, on the whole, adapting themselves successfully to the requirements of a rapidly advancing technology it could simultaneously be true that they are also moving away from the good life. The possibility that in the process of becoming more productive men will unavoidably become less articulate and sensitive – though content to remain so – cannot be excluded.

I happen to believe, however, that men have not so far been remarkably successful in adapting themselves to the new 'runaway world' that is emerging. Casual evidence suggests the contrary; that technological momentum is maintained at an excessive cost in terms of nervous strain, frustration and despondency. This, at any rate, is the theme of Part V, though I make no claim to have presented there a balanced picture.

Nor is there any immediate call for a balanced picture in this respect. Since there is no present danger of the alleged benefits of growth being understated by the scientists or technocrats, who today have the public ear prior to taking over the earth tomorrow, we have become accustomed to having the picture of human prospects painted in bright and glowing tints. I have applied myself without compunction, therefore, to daubing in the black spots.

I shall not pretend that the task has been uncongenial, and there may well be places where the flow of ideas and feeling has carried the argument beyond a point that can be comfortably sustained by reason alone. On the whole, however, I think the incursion into this faintly charted territory has been worth while if only for the opportunity it afforded of giving systematic expression to my own misgivings about the sort of world that technology is shaping for us. But I also entertain the hope that, on putting the book down, some readers may be persuaded to contemplate the future with less complacency than when they took it up.

Part I

Economics: Necessity or Choice?

Chapter 1

Growthmania

I

Revolutions from below break out not when material circumstances are oppressive but, according to a popular historical generalization, when they are improving and hope of a better life is in the air. So long as toil and hardship was the rule for the mass of people over countless centuries, so long as economic activity was viewed as a daily struggle against the niggardliness of nature, men were resigned to eke out a living by the sweat of their brows untroubled by visions of ease and plenty. And although economic growth was not unheard of before this century – certainly the eighteenth century economists had a lively awareness of the opportunities for economic expansion, through innovation, through trade and through the division of labour – it was not until the recent post-war recovery turned into a period of sustained economic advance for the West, and the latest products of technological innovation were everywhere visible, and audible, that countries rich and poor became aware of a new phenomenon in the calendar of events, since watched everywhere with intentness and anxiety, the growth index.[1] While his father thought himself fortunate to be decently employed, the European worker today expresses resentment if his attention is drawn to any lag of his earnings behind those of other occupations. If, before the war, the nation was thankful for a prosperous year, today it is urged to chafe and fret on discovering that other nations have done perhaps better yet.

Indeed with the establishment of the National Economic Development Council in 1962 economic growth has become an official feature of

[1] Like a national flag and a national airline, a national plan for economic growth is deemed an essential item in the paraphernalia of every new nation state.

3

the Establishment. To be *with* growth is manifestly to be 'with it' and, like speed itself, the faster the better. And if NEDC, or 'Neddy' as it is affectionately called, is to be superseded, it will be only to make way for larger and more forceful neddies. In the meantime every business-man, politician, city editor or writer, impatient to acquire a reputation for economic sagacity and no-nonsense realism is busy shouting giddy-up in several of two-score different ways. If the country was ever un-certain of the ends it should pursue, that day has passed. There may be doubts among philosophers and heart-searchings among poets, but to the multitude the kingdom of God is to be realized here, and now, on this earth; and it is to be realized via technological innovation, and at an exponential rate. Its universal appeal exceeds that of the brotherhood of man, indeed it comprehends it. For as we become richer, surely we shall remedy all social evils; heal the sick, comfort the aged and exhilarate the young. One has only to think with sublime credulity of the oppor-tunities to be opened to us by the harvest of increasing wealth: universal adult education, free art and entertainment, frequent visits to the moon, a domesticated robot in every home and, therefore, woman forever freed from drudgery; for the common man, a lifetime of leisure to pursue culture and pleasure (or, rather, to absorb them from the TV screen); for the scientists, ample funds to devise increasingly powerful and ingenious computers so that we may have yet more time for culture and pleasure and scientific discovery.

Here, then, is the panacea to be held with a fervour, indeed with a piety, that silences thought. What conceivable alternative could there be to economic growth? Explicit references to it are hardly necessary. When the Prime Minister talks with exaltation of a 'sense of national purpose' it goes without saying that he is inspired by a vision, a cornucopia of burgeoning indices.

But to be tediously logical about it, there is an alternative to the post-war growth-rush as an overriding objective of economic policy: the simple alternative, that is, of not rushing for growth. The alternative is intended to be taken seriously. One may concede the importance of economic growth in an indigent society, in a country with an outsize population wherein the mass of people struggle for bare subsistence. But despite ministerial twaddle about the efforts we must make to 'survive in a competitive world', Britain is just not that sort of country. Irrespective of its 'disappointing' rate of growth, or the present position of the gold reserves, it may be reasonably regarded, in view of its productive capacity and skills, as one of the more affluent societies of the West, a country with a wide margin of choice in its policy objectives. And it is palpably absurd to continue talking, and acting, as if our survival – or our 'economic health' – depended upon that extra one or two per cent growth. At the risk of offending financial journalists and other fastidious scrutinizers of economic statistics, whose spirits have been trained to soar or sink on detecting a half per cent swing in any index, I must voice the view that the near-exclusive concern with industrial growth is, in the present condition of Britain, unimaginative and unworthy.

The reader, however, may be more inclined to concede this point and to ponder on a more discriminating criterion of economic policy if he is reminded of some of the less laudable consequences of economic growth over the last twenty years.

Undergraduate economists learn in their first year that the private enterprise system is a marvellous mechanism. By their third year, it is to be hoped, they have come to learn also that there is a great deal it cannot do, and much that it does very badly. For today's generation in particular, it is a fact of experience that within the span of a few years the unlimited marketing of new technological products can result in a cumulative reduction of the pleasure once freely enjoyed by the citizen. If there is one clear policy alternative to pressing on regardless, it is the policy of seeking immediate remedies against the rapid spread of disamenities that now beset the daily lives of ordinary people. More positively, there is the alternative policy of transferring resources from industrial production to the more urgent task of transforming the physical environment in which we live into something less fit for machines, perhaps, but more fit for human beings.

Since I shall illustrate particular abuses of unchecked commercialism in later chapters and criticize them on grounds familiar to economists, I refrain from elaboration at this point. However, it is impossible not to dwell for a moment on the most notorious by-product of industrialization the world has ever known: the appalling traffic congestion in our towns, cities and suburbs. It is at this phenomenon that our political leaders should look for a really outstanding example of post-war growth. One consequence is that the pleasures of strolling along the streets of a city are more of a memory than a current pastime. Lorries, motor-cycles and taxis belching fumes, filth and stench, snarling engines and unabating visual disturbance have compounded to make movement through the city an ordeal for the pedestrian at the same time as the mutual strangulation of the traffic makes it a purgatory for motorists. The formula of mend-and-make-do followed by successive transport ministers is culminating in a maze of one-way streets, peppered with parking meters, with massive signs, detours, and weirdly shaped junctions and circuses across which traffic pours from several directions, while penned-in pedestrians jostle each other along narrow pavements. Think, for instance, of Piccadilly Circus, the hub of a capital city, imprisoned in its traffic.

Towns and cities have been rapidly transmogrified into roaring workshops, the authorities watching anxiously as the traffic builds up with no policy other than that of spreading the rash of parking meters to discourage the traffic on the one hand, and, on the other, to accommodate it by road-widening, tunnelling, bridging and patching up here and there; perverting every principle of amenity a city can offer in the attempt to force through it the growing traffic. This 'policy' – apparently justified by reckoning as social benefits any increase in the volume of traffic and any increase in its average speed – would, if it were pursued more ruthlessly, result inevitably in a Los Angeles-type solution in which the greater part of the metropolis is converted to road space; in effect a city buried under roads and freeways. The once-mooted alternative, a Buchanan-type plan – 'traffic architecture' based on the principle of multi-level separating of motorized traffic and pedestrians – may be an improvement compared with the present drift into chaos, but it would take decades to implement, would cost the earth, and would apparently remove us from contact with it. The more radical solution of prohibiting private traffic from town and city centres, resorts, and places of recreation, can be confidently expected to meet with the organized hostility of the motoring interests and 'friends of freedom'. Yet, short of dismembering our towns and cities, there is no feasible alternative to increasing constraints on the freedom of private vehicles.

II

Other disagreeable features may be mentioned in passing, many of them the result either of wide-eyed enterprise or of myopic municipalities, such as the post-war 'development' blight, the erosion of the countryside, the 'uglification' of coastal towns, the pollution of the air[1]

[1]According to Professor L. J. Battan, of Arizona, *The Unclean Sky: A*

and of rivers with chemical wastes, the accumulation of thick oils on our coastal waters, the sewage poisoning our beaches, the destruction of wild life by the indiscriminate use of pesticides, the change-over from animal farming to animal factories and, visible to all who have eyes to see, a rich heritage of natural beauty being wantonly destroyed – a heritage that cannot be restored in our lifetime.

For it is the unprecedented speed and scale of developments that have caught us off our guard. Such is the expanding power of modern technology, such the opportunism of man's enterprise, that the disposal of the waste products of industry, which for thousands of years were absorbed into the cycle of nature, have suddenly, it seems, broken all ecological bounds. And the general public, its attention continually distracted by technological wonders, has simply no notion of the extent or gravity of the situation. It does not, therefore, stop to reflect on the generations it would take to undo the damage wrought over the last half century; to regrow forests on the hundreds of thousands of acres stripped of timber, to remove some of the thousands of square miles of concrete laid over the earth, to purify lakes and rivers reeking of sewage, to revive the wild life of Africa, to restore to its original magnificence several thousand miles of Mediterranean coastline ruined in the post-war tourist spree, to cleanse the atmosphere of millions of tons of floating pollutants and of the uncertain but growing amount of radioactive matter.

If anything, one detects an 'eat, drink, and be merry spirit' abroad, inadvertently perhaps fostered by the historian whose cultivated detachment forbids him to be ruffled by current events. Rather than project uncouth magnitudes into the future, it is simpler to respond to present dangers by observing patiently that similar alarms were sounded in ages gone by. Did not Malthus warn the world of the mounting pressure of population at the close of the eighteenth century – when population was a small fraction of what it is now? Science, like love, will surely find a way! And the disappearance of the countryside? Go back a century, and we shall also find men lamenting the vanishing countryside! Go

---

Meteorologist looks at Air Pollution, the air above is treated as a vast sewer. Gases have been poured into the atmosphere in the mistaken belief that the wind, like a river, would not only carry the wastes away but somehow purify them in the process. As a result, some ten million tons of solid pollutants are now floating around in the sky. There is, however, a limit to what the finite atmosphere can safely disperse: what goes up must eventually come down.

back to the eighteenth century, or farther back to the seventeenth, and always we shall find men who, despising the new towns, bemoan the passing of the rustic virtues! *Ergo*, nothing has really changed; all alarm is groundless. This time-hallowed anti-Jeremaid ploy was particularly in evidence after the explosion of the two atomic bombs over Japan in 1945. Some readers may recall a particular cartoon representing a conversation between two cave-men watching a third walking away with a rough-hewn stone axe. The caption read: 'With this dreadful new weapon that Smith has invented, the survival of mankind itself is in the greatest danger.' Find a precedent, invent a precedent if needs be, and, apparently, the danger is effectively exorcized!

III

Our political leaders, all of them, have visited the United States, and all of them seem to have learned the wrong things. They have been impressed by the efficient organization of industry, the high productivity, the extent of automation, and the new one-plane, two-yacht, three-car, four-television-set family. The spreading suburban wilderness, the near traffic paralysis, the mixture of pandemonium and desolation in the cities, a sense of spiritual despair scarcely concealed by the frantic pace of life – such phenomena, not being readily quantifiable, and having no discernible impact on the gold reserves, are obviously not regarded as agenda.

Indeed, the jockeying among party leaders for recognition as the agents of modernization, of the new, the bigger and better, is one of the sadder facts of the post-war world, in particular as their claim to the title rests almost wholly on a propensity to keep their eyes glued to the speedometer without regard to the direction taken. Our environment is sinking fast into a welter of disamenities, yet the most vocal part of the community cannot raise their eyes from the trade figures to remark the painful event. Too many of us try not to notice it, or if occasionally we feel sick or exasperated we tend to shrug in resignation. We hear a lot about 'the costs of progress', and since the productivity figures over the years tend to rise we assume that on balance, and, in some sense, we must be better off.

In the endeavour to arrest this mass flight from reality into statistics I hope to persuade the reader that the chief sources of social welfare are to be found not in economic growth *per se* but in a more selective form of development, one that includes a radical reshaping of our physical environment with the needs of civilized living – and not the needs of motorized traffic or industry – foremost in mind. Indeed, in the later chapters it will be observed that the social accommodation to technological advance is, in any case, almost sure to reduce our experience of welfare.

Before launching into the main themes, however, something must be said about the widespread misconception which persuades us that, as a nation, we have no real choice: that living in the twentieth century we are compelled to do all sorts of things we might otherwise not wish to do. Since childhood, I imagine, all too many of us have lived in awe of the balance of payments. And now that economic growth is all the rage we have come unthinkingly to link faster economic growth with the prospect of improved trade figures, a proposition for which there is no economic warrant.

Enough will be said in the next two chapters to show that there is a great deal more choice in our domestic affairs and in the conduct of our foreign trade than is usually conveyed in the financial columns of the press; at least enough to free us from the imagined compulsion to expand rapidly and from popular bogies of 'not surviving' or of 'being left behind in the race', or of 'stagnating in an amiable backwater'.

Chapter 2

The No-choice Misconception

I

Let us begin by being platitudinous to the point of remarking that of three possible goals of long-term policy (1) economic growth, (2) a more equitable distribution of the national product, and (3) improved allocation of our national resources, all three play some part in the complex of existing economic policy. Differences of opinion may therefore be attributed to differences in emphasis. For many years now the emphasis has been almost entirely on growth, whereas one of the themes of this essay is that it ought to be almost entirely on improving the allocation of our existing resources. It is the task of these first chapters to persuade the reader of the urgent need for this shift in priorities.

Before inspecting these long-term goals more closely, let us distinguish them from the perennial concerns of the day-to-day running of the country which too often appear wholly to absorb the energies of the Government. These routine preoccupations, which go to fill the financial columns of our newspapers and are the subject of innumerable reports, are three in number: (*a*) the maintenance of a high level of employment; (*b*) the stabilization of the level of prices; and (*c*) the promotion of a favourable balance of payments. In so far as we succeed in these objectives we refer to the economy as 'healthy' or, better yet, 'sound'. Certainly it would be reckless to ignore the indices of the current performance of the economy. Any time that (*a*) a large proportion of the voluntary labour force is without employment; or (*b*) an initially suppressed inflation has slipped its restraints and a distrust of the currency is speading; or (*c*) there is no reasonable prospect of paying for the inflow of goods from abroad, a sense of crisis impends and there is warrant enough for temporarily overlooking long-term goals in the immediate attempt to return the economy to a more acceptable norm in any of these respects. The economy may be likened to an engine whose smooth functioning is indicated by governors labelled 'employment', 'price stability' and 'balance of payments'. Obviously any poor performance calls for repairs; and it is the task of a good mechanic to avoid breakdowns and ensure the good condition of the engine. But keeping the engine trouble-free is not an end in itself. The engine drives a vehicle, and the speed of the vehicle to some extent, and the direction it takes, to a greater extent – long-term policies – are what really matter.

Since national self-castigation, in all economic matters at least, has been in high fashion since the war, one must risk the charge of unpardonable complacency by the reflection that our post-war record has been good enough compared with those of other countries. We have enjoyed a very high level of employment (some economists would say too high) and though in consequence prices have indeed risen they have not risen at a dangerous speed. The balance of payments position, though frequently troublesome, is not intractable and may be resolved by a variety of measures none of which is likely to cause any great hardship. Our growth rates, as we all know, appear near the bottom of the international league table. But if we can bear to live with this mortifying fact,[1] we can still live comfortably. None the less the attention paid to these popular indicators of 'economic health' is excessive when compared with any critical analysis of our long-term plans. An explanation of the popularity of this sort of 'index economics', especially among financial journalists, may well be that an aptitude for summarizing official figures, for the uttering of grave warnings whenever there is a down-turn in the graphs, is not a difficult one to pick up.

The knowledge that several hundred financial journalists and government officials pursue this hobby – tabulate figures (to the nearest million), construct charts, and spin endless columns of verbal statistics – is something we might continue to put up with were it not for the fact that the fascination with index economics detracts attention from

[1] Not every kind of growth index, however, would place Britain near the bottom of the list. Much would depend upon the base period adopted, the length of the period chosen, the goods included and their relative weights in the index. If frequent tea-breaks and other manifestations of disguised leisure are regarded as *goods* – and economics suggests they be so regarded – their conceivable quantification and inclusion in any index of output *per capita* might go some way to enhance Britain's comparative performance.

the broader aims of economic policy, and tends to become a substitute for them. We become so preoccupied with the ups and downs of the indices that we fail to raise our sights to the larger issues that confront us. Continuously arguing about and tinkering with the economic engine, we have only afterthoughts to spare for the rapid and visible changes taking place about us. In the event, there is no general awareness by the public of the range of significant social choices facing it.

Admittedly the economic engine has not been turning very smoothly for some time, but the trouble is, in the last resort, more political than economic.

In a bid to capture public support successive governments have gone out of their way, over the last fifteen years, to implant expectations of rising incomes and opportunities. More recently, official support of arbitrary growth targets has as much as invited annual wage-claims by the trade unions. Having so assiduously sown the seeds of rising expectations we are reaping the harvest of rising prices. A slow but uninterrupted inflation over the last quarter of a century has imparted to the economy a psychological momentum: workers, managers, bankers, professional men, shareholders, all anticipate rising incomes and prices to continue over the future notwithstanding anything governments may do.

The political commitment to a fixed parity for sterling and to support for a level of employment that is evidently well within the inflationary zone, however, makes it risky for governments to do the obvious things – introduce effective flexibility into the price of sterling and into monetary policy. They have turned, instead, with singular lack of success, to increased reliance on fancy fiscal measures, to dramatic announcements of changes in Bank Rate, and to brave but ineffectual ministerial speeches exhorting us to work harder and export more, all of which give greater impetus to the preoccupation with index economics and to dilletantism among financial journalists.

I cannot see this country in the near future freeing itself from the exhausting preoccupation with the internal and external value of its currency, and from drifting from one petty crisis to another – and, therefore, among the endless bickering and hullabaloo, neglecting the growing disamenities about us and the consequent urgency of revising our long-term economic policy to deal with them – (1) unless the Government is ready to make more frequent and more drastic changes in the money supply, and to accustom businessmen to respond without con-

sternation to wider and more frequent movements in Bank Rate and
security prices;[1] (2) unless the Government is prepared to see the employment figure decline below the 98 per cent level;[2] and (3) unless the
Government is prepared to promote flexibility in the price of sterling to
enable us to determine our domestic policy, primarily and for all times,
by reference to the domestic situation and not, as at present, primarily
by reference to the state of our foreign exchange reserves.

It does not seem self-evident to me that if the need for these measures
were put fairly to the public they would be rejected. But even if they
were received, initially, with ill grace, they should – at least if we
believe in their efficacy – be brought continuously to the attention of
the public. In view of this desideratum it is discouraging, though perhaps
not surprising, to observe that whenever the economist gets too close to
the machinery of government he is all too prone to talk the language of
'political feasibility'. In order to avoid frustration he may learn to advocate only those measures he believes stand some chance of acceptance.
This implies, however, failure to advocate technically efficient measures
for fear of being ignored by governments whose range of policies is
limited by party ideology, financial shibboleths and public prejudice.
But once the economist succumbs to the easy habit of making only those

[1]There is one non-political argument against the vigorous use of monetary
policy – a policy that entails more frequent and more drastic (though less
dramatic) changes in Bank Rate and also in the supply of money – vigorous
enough to exert the required pressure notwithstanding the high liquidity of the
private sector: the instability argument. If monetary policy is used as timidly
as it is currently being used, then it will continue to be ineffective. If, on the other
hand, the measures taken are drastic enough to be effective they will, it is suggested, be too effective; i.e. once the pressure begins to tell it will send the
economy into a downward spin. The strong measures required to correct this
downward movement will, in its turn, 'overshoot the mark' and send the
economy soaring into inflation.

If this were a fact of economic life we might well despair of deflecting the
economy from the path of perpetual inflation. But though it is a common
view, and one that lends support to those who would avoid politically unpopular measures, there is just no evidence to support it. Indeed, in an economy
in which changes in Bank Rate and in the money supply are infrequent and
limited, the data necessary for testing this peculiar instability hypothesis do not
exist. In these frustrating circumstances there is much to be said for bolder
experiments with monetary measures.

[2]We may have to learn to live with the unpalatable social fact that (at least
in a non-totalitarian society) price stability requires x per cent unemployment
on the average, where x is greater than two. This may not be unbearable if the
turnover of the unemployed pool is fairly rapid and, also, if substantial increases
in unemployment pay come into force.

recommendations that accord with 'political realities' he soon finds
himself in the uncomfortable position of using his authority to sanction
the political fashions of the day.

II

There is, however, one more reason why we have failed to take the
straightforward measures referred to, preferring instead to tinker with
a ragbag of fiscal devices, and this is the popular belief that faster
growth is the real solution to our chronic economic infirmities. If only
we can 'get Britain moving', presumably at the official 3½ per cent
growth rate, inflation would cease to plague us and our balance of
payments problems would cease. Indeed, there is a two-way connection
here: if faster economic growth is believed by some to enable us to
overcome the problems posed by excess imports and rising prices, the
same people are also apt to believe that success in increasing exports
and stabilizing prices improves the prospects for economic growth.
Thus, if we are all of us opposed to 'stop-go' policies, it is not because
the excitement is too much for us; not even because they cause great
hardship in themselves, but because these periodic reversals of monetary
and fiscal measures taken by successive governments are believed to be
detrimental to sustained economic growth. If we worry about creeping
inflation, it is not so much because of its inequitable distributional
effects as for fear of losing exports. And, as indicated, there are many
who believe that increased exports is both a pre-condition and an effect
of increased economic growth.

   This is the circle of reasoning within which we have been confined
during the last decade or so and which is predominant in official
quarters. It is a circle of reasoning that seems to leave us little choice.
We appear to be caught in a treadmill, wherein we must press harder
if we are to 'keep up in the race', or even to survive. Yet, if the truth
must be told, there is no economic warrant for such constricting beliefs.
We have only ourselves to blame if our no-nonsense patriots have
mesmerized us over the years into this unrelenting frame of mind.

   With the rapid growth in the popular channels of communication it
is more true than ever before that the sheer weight of reiteration rather
than the power of reason influences the attitude of the public. A simple
term such as 'growth potential' is loaded with compulsion: it suggests
that waste is incurred whenever we fail, as invariably we do, to realize

this potential growth. It is a term apt to the technocratic view of things, that envisages the country as some sort of vast power-house with every grown man and woman a potential unit of input to be harnessed to a generating system from which flows this vital stuff called industrial output. And since this stuff can be measured statistically as GNP (Gross National Product) it follows that the more of it the better. Viewed as power-houses for producing GNP certain countries appear to perform better than Britain. It is obvious, therefore, that we must make every endeavour to catch up. Moreover, other countries use more engineers and more PhD's per million of population than we do. Also they have a higher productivity. It follows that we *need x* per cent more engineers and *y* per cent more PhD's. To continue, steel output could, if we tried hard, rise to *z* million tons by 1970, as much *per capita* as the US has now. In consequence, we *need* to expand steel capacity at *w* per cent per annum. Again, in order for every family in Britain to have its own motor-car by 1975 we need to expand the motor-car industry at *v* per cent per annum. With such 'needs of industry' to be met we shall require increased commercial transport and, therefore, increased imports of fuel. Consequently we *need* to work harder in order to pay for our *needs*. And so we go on, slipping from implicit choices to explicit imperatives.

It would be futile, of course, to suggest that we should be thinking about the possibilities of reducing the working day. After all, in the US, where productivity per man-hour is said to be about twice our own, people do not appear to be enjoying more leisure.[1] How could we possibly hope to compete in world markets? What choice have we but to return to the treadmill?

This is a sad state for any nation to be in, and in an affluent society surpassingly strange. Having come this far into the twentieth century with economists interpreting the alleged increase in our real income as 'enrichment' or, more sagaciously, as 'an extention of the area of choice', and then to be told almost daily that we have no choice; that if we are to pay our way in the world we must work harder than ever. This is enough surely to tax the credulity of any being whose judgement has not yet been swept away by torrents of economic exhortation.

But of course we have a choice, a wide range of choice! The main

[1] In this connection see T. Scitovsky 'What Price Economic Progress', *Yale Review*, 1959 (reprinted in *Papers on Welfare and Growth*, Allen & Unwin, London, 1964).

purpose of this essay is to uncover the kinds of choices that face us, or any modern community, and to make it apparent that the so-called policy of economic growth as popularly understood is hardly more than a policy of drifting quickly – of snatching at any technological innovation that proves marketable with scant respect for the social consequences.

In the formulation of the ends of economic policy the word *need* is not to be invoked. Markets do not *need* to expand – although, of course, businessmen dearly like to see them expand (whether through increasing *per capita* income, increasing domestic population or increased immigration). It is quite possible to arrange things so as to produce a good deal fewer gadgets and instead to enjoy more leisure. And, although blasphemous to utter, it is also possible to train fewer scientists and engineers without our perishing from the face of the earth. Nor do we *need* to capture world markets in the hope of being able to lower costs; or to lower costs in the hope of capturing world markets. We can, while acting as rational beings, deliberately choose to reduce our foreign trade and in some lines, therefore, to produce smaller quantities at a somewhat higher cost. We can cut down on newspaper advertisements and preserve forestlands.[1] We can decide even to reduce the strains of com-

[1] The manufacturer of newspaper consumes whole forests. Every Sunday issue of *The New York Times* devours the product of 150 acres. In this connection see Robert Arvill, *Man and Environment* (Chapter 2) (1967). If there were some institutional mechanism offering buyers of *The New York Times* the alternative choice, one Sunday, of a jointly held area of 150 acres of forestland for their future recreation, they might well choose the latter.

Why are such choices not offered to people? The market is a low-cost mechanism only for individually produced goods, such as watches, wallpaper, cars and thimbles. Goods which simultaneously benefit a large number of people, so-called 'collective goods' such as street drains, parks, museums, city illumination and public works, present difficulties both in the decisions necessary to produce them and to price their services once produced. For lack of an effective mechanism of choice, decisions about the creation of public goods tend to be made by governments which, in deference to taxpayers, are generally guided by narrow pecuniary principles.

On this system of reaching decisions about the creation of public goods it is almost certain that collective goods which promote the quality of life, handsome boulevards, parks, attractive city centres, could add penny for penny far more satisfaction to our lives than much of the individual frippery we should never think of buying were it not for their persistent advertising. But until we can evolve an effective low-cost mechanism for determining the maximum sums each family in the community is prepared to pay to share in the benefits of a wide range of such collective goods, their potential benefit will tend to remain under-exploited.

The implications of this important thesis are cogently argued in Kenneth Galbraith's *The Affluent Society*, and calls for no elaboration in these pages.

petition and opt for an easier and more leisurely life. Such choices as these, and many others also, can be translated into perfectly practicable alternatives whenever public opinion is ready to consider them. But not before, since such choices will not be presented to us by the working of the market.

In the meantime, though one cannot object to the orthodox school's dubbing all suggested alternatives to the sweat-and-strain doctrine as irresponsible, it would be a service to the community if they forsook the word *need* in favour of the word *want*. So simple a switch of words would act to remind us that policies radically different from those we habitually pursue are open to us all the time – though some people may feel uncertain of, or disapprove of, some of their consequences.

III

Appendix A on the balance of payments is written for the reader who is still the victim of the common but vague notion that the pressures of world competition virtually compel us to treat economic growth as a top priority. It may be left out on a first reading, however, as it forms something of a digression from the mainstream of the argument. Needless to say, my sympathies are with the ordinary citizen who can hardly fail to be influenced by the disproportionate attention paid to foreign trade in our newspapers, and who is subjected mercilessly to fallacious official pronouncements such as that requiring us to work harder if we are 'to pay our way in the world', or that which lays it down that unless we grow faster we shall run further into international debt, or become insolvent.

Misconceptions such as these render the public more vulnerable to monotonous chorus of the orthodox school, that we have no choice but to thrust ahead at all cost. They make the public more tolerant, therefore, of those growing disamenities that have resulted from a tacit acceptance of purely commercial criteria within the existing legal framework.

Chapter 3

The Choices Open to Us

I

In the light of the preceding remarks let us reconsider the question of emphasis among three components of long-term economic policy:

(1) *Economic Growth.* Though no economist who has studied the relation between economics and social welfare would endorse a policy of economic growth without an embarrassing amount of qualification, the profession as a whole behaves as if, on balance, it was a good thing. This attitude may spring from an impatience with quasi-philosophical inquiries that unavoidably call into question the usefulness of much of the highly skilled economic research currently undertaken. But there is room also for rationalization. One of the more obvious pretexts for pressing on regardless is the existence of poverty in the greater part of the world: in Asia, in Africa, and in large parts of South America. There are pockets of degrading poverty even within the wealthy countries though, as indicated earlier, their continuation may be attributed ultimately to political prejudices, not to economic necessity.[1]

Now if the rich countries, in response to a moral challenge, sought to convert themselves into an arsenal to provision the hungry areas of Asia and Africa, a case could be made for retaining economic growth as the chief goal of economic policy for some considerable time. But though

[1] If within these wealthy countries the public conscience is unperturbed by the existence of a small minority of very poor people, many of whom are too old or too sick to take care of themselves, we might as well admit it. It is hypocrisy to pretend that the only way to help them is to create more wealth by growing faster when, in fact, the share of the under-privileged minority in the annual increment of output is negligible.

magniloquence on the foreign aid theme marks all fitting occasions, the scale of such aid to poor countries in the post-war period is more suggestive, to use Professor Bauer's words, of 'conscience money' than of moral commitment. When we bear in mind that the total aid given to poor countries by the largest donor, the United States, a country that is struggling continuously with problems of near-surfeit, does not amount to as much as one per cent of its Gross National Product, one has no choice but to reject this justification out of hand.[1]

The belief that only a faster economic growth will enable any country to 'pay its way in the world', or that faster growth generates more exports, does not stand up to analysis. The purpose of Appendix A on the balance of payments is to convince the reader of this allegation and to make him aware of a number of misconceptions about foreign trade.

Again, the belief that the nation's security from military attack is strengthened by faster economic growth is unacceptable to the economist whose training disposes him to reject so unsophisticated a view. If it were felt that the country's chance of repelling a hostile force in the next few years would be improved by augmenting our weapons supply or advancing our war technology, either could be achieved more directly by shifting a larger proportion of our resources into the required activity. Nevertheless, though few would regard it as the main justification of a faster rate of economic growth, this question of national defence deserves to be treated in a little more detail – as in fact it is in Appendix B.

We fall back then on the more popular and explicit belief that a *per capita* rise in real income is a good thing in itself; that in expanding the range of opportunities for ordinary people it increases their welfare. It will not, however, be difficult to uncover serious weaknesses in this common presumption, enough at any rate to warrant a conclusion that

[1] The limited ability of these poor countries to absorb aid and the balance of payments problem are sometimes invoked to explain the glaringly inadequate contribution of the West. Neither factor carries conviction. There may indeed be difficulties of persuading indigenous populations to use Western techniques and of training them to operate modern machinery. But there should be no difficulty in supplying the direct needs of people – foodstuffs, clothing, medical supplies, pesticides, contraceptives and farm implements – in order to alleviate distress. As for the balance-of-payments problem, if the US guaranteed to provide, say, 10 per cent of its annual income to India, that country would be glad to accept it as a tied gift – that is, subject to the condition that the dollars received be spent entirely in the USA.

economic growth *per se* is a component of policy on which the least emphasis should be placed if we are interested primarily in social welfare.

Indices of economic growth may measure, in a rough sort of way, the increase in a country's gross productive power. But no provision is made in such indices for the 'negative goods' that are also being increased; that is, for the increasing burden of disamenities in the country. Nor can they reveal certain imponderable but none the less crucial consequences associated with the indiscriminate pursuit of technological progress, about which something will be said in the last part of this book. Indeed, the adoption of economic growth as a primary aim of policy, whether it is urged upon us as a moral duty to the rest of the world or as a duty to posterity, or as a condition of survival, seems on reflection as likely to add, at least, as much 'ill-fare' as welfare to society. Certainly there can be no purely economic justification for a policy of growth *per se*. The simple view that it 'enrichens' society, or that it expands the range of choice open to mankind, stands up neither to argument nor to the facts of common experience – unless, of course, words such as 'enrichen' or 'expanding choices' are made to carry the same meaning as an increase of productive potential which is, roughly, what the index of productivity seeks to measure. If, however, we are concerned with social welfare in the ordinary sense, the only legitimate procedure is to consider consequences of each and every economic reorganization entailed by the growth process, in the endeavour to determine which, on balance, are beneficial and which are not. It may justly be protested that this is impracticable; that we cannot foretell the consequences, tangible and intangible, of the economic and social reorganizations resulting from a succession of interdependent technological innovations. However, we can make some attempt to sort things out. We may put aside until later some general reflections on certain potent albeit intangible factors, and in the meantime consider the sorts of welfare criteria by which economists have sought to justify the adoption of one policy as against alternative policies. The scope for such criteria is admittedly restricted, as we shall presently see, but the notions on which they are raised help to orient our thinking. Moreover, in circumstances where their application may be admitted, they can be very revealing. In particular, they enable us to point up some of the chief sources of 'ill-fare' that remain uncorrected under present institutions.

Indeed, we might go so far as to suggest that economic growth *per se* should be jettisoned as an independent goal of policy. For if we are concerned primarily with social welfare, those forms of economic growth that meet our welfare criteria will in any case be approved and adopted, the remainder being rejected: thus, sources of 'worthwhile' economic growth will continue to be sought after.

II

(2) *A more equal distribution of real income* has long been recognized by Western societies as one of the chief aims of economic policy. While, in general, any change in the pattern of prices – either of goods and/or of productive services – makes some people better and others worse off, the most effective short run method for redistributing real income is the levying of highly progressive income taxes and capital taxes, while making freely available to all the greater number of services provided by the Government.

On the assumption that the structure of ability in the UK is more equally distributed than the structure of disposable incomes, the existing policies for expanding educational opportunities have long run effects in equalizing earning power. Since so much is already being done in Britain along these lines, it would be useful, before moving on, to take stock of our present position.

As Professor Titmuss has pointed out,[1] the official statistics available are unreliable in so many respects that any conclusion about the trend of income distribution over the last two decades must be treated with a degree of caution that effectively forbids any presumption one way or the other. The common impression that there is greater social and economic equality today than there was, say, in the thirties, is formed from several developments: (*a*) the extension to every employed person since 1948 of national insurance and the provision of a national health service covering every person in the country. Today over 40 per cent of the Government's current expenditure is on social services, compared with about a quarter in 1920; and this over a period that has seen public expenditure increase from 20 per cent of the net national expenditure to something approaching 50 per cent. (*b*) A rise in the average standard of living since the war of about 45 per cent (in terms of disposable real income) – much of this economic gain taking tangible shape as a widespread ownership of consumer durables such as motor-cars, washing

[1] R. M. Titmuss, *Income Distribution and Social Change* (Allen & Unwin. London, 1963).

machines, television sets, refrigerators, vacuum cleaners, and the like.
(c) The maintenance during the post-war period of a high level of
employment with unusually good opportunities for unskilled and
juvenile labour – an era that seems to be coming to a close. (d) A
gradual extension to all social groups in the community of higher
education over the last two decades. The student population today is
running at about a quarter of a million compared with some sixty
thousand before the war, and the numbers are expected to rise rapidly
over the next decade.

For all that, existing inequality of wealth still appears quite striking.
According to Professor Meade,[1] the top one per cent of income recipients in 1959 took about 12 per cent of the total national income; they
also accounted for nearly 50 per cent of the country's total income from
property. The top 5 per cent took about a quarter of the national income, and about two-thirds of the total income from property. None the
less, the inspiration towards a greater degree of equalization does not, or
should not, draw its strength only from a sense of unfairness, or envy on
contemplating the figures at the top end of the scale. After all, one can
envisage a society having a small proportion of very rich families, withal
a comfortable standard of living for the remainder. This is not the
condition in Britain, however. Despite the extention of welfare services
and the increase in pensions and unemployment benefit since the war,
the position at the lower end of the scale is anything but reassuring. The
official income figures are not very helpful since the breakdown is by
person and not by family, and many of the poor do not earn any income
in the official sense. But we do know that during the last two years[2]
some two million people, at any one time, were receiving support from
the National Assistance Board, the bulk of them old age pensioners, to
say nothing of an estimated 200,000 more who were eligible but who did
not apply for assistance. Bearing in mind that the maximum earnings of
a husband and wife receiving such assistance cannot be much more than
£5 a week; bearing in mind further that, of the remainder of the six
million pensioners (entitled to £3 7s. 6d. for a single person and £5 9s. od.
for a married couple) many of them have little more than their pensions
to live on; and, finally comparing these figures with the average *per*

[1] J. E. Meade, *Efficiency, Equality and the Ownership of Property* (Allen &
Unwin. London, 1964).
[2] 1964–5.

capita earnings of the working population of about £18 a week,[1] one cannot escape the conclusion that a substantial degree of poverty and hardship for old people lingers on in the so-called welfare state of this affluent society.

In order to make a dent in this problem, a sum of the order of about half a billion pounds a year would have to be transferred to the underprivileged group – about 2 per cent of our national income. On the face of things, an income transfer of this magnitude is rather formidable, though not impracticable on economic grounds given the political will. Indeed, it is something less than the average annual increase of our national income. A reduction of our defence budget to about three-quarters of the present estimate would suffice to provide it. If no reduction of government expenditure took place, however, it would require an addition in the first year of between two shillings and two-and-sixpence to the standard rate to raise the sum, though less than this if capital gains were taxed at the same rate as income.

Putting aside the methods of dealing with this urgent problem of hard core poverty, and turning to the condition of the community at large (less this special category), one might hazard a guess that the movement towards increasing equality of wealth will continue for some time as the advantages of being born into wealth are increasingly offset by the educational opportunities being opened to young people irrespective of income or social group. The one major contingency that could upset these sanguine expectations is that of an unemployment crisis within the next few years caused by the rapid adoption of automation in industry and commerce. Looking beyond such crises and farther into the future in which such educational policies as we are now pursuing will have established a thoroughgoing meritocracy – one in which those born into talent, instead of into wealth, will be rewarded with top positions, and those found wanting will be relegated to the bottom of the hierarchy – one cannot be sure whether gross or disposable income and wealth will be more equally distributed than they are today. But there is no reason to suppose that the resulting income inequalities, which will tend to reflect the unmerited fact of being born into talent rather than into wealth, would come to be regarded as more tolerable.

A far simpler alternative, however, and one which should have

---

[1] These figures are for 1964-5. Since 29th March, 1966, the pension has been raised to £4 for a single person and £6 10s. for a married couple. Earnings *per capita* in 1965-6 were closer to £19 a week.

more immediate appeal would involve no more than a reallocation of some part of our annual public expenditure on welfare services, currently running at the rate of about £7 billion. The prevailing principle of universality of benefits presents every retired earner with a State pension though, obviously, not each of them needs a State pension. In fact, about every other couple receiving a State pension has (according to the 1966 Pension Survey) an income of £10 a week or more. The State, also, is prepared to finance every child's schooling. Yet a considerable proportion of the families whose children's schooling is so financed would be quite able and willing, if necessary, to pay the full cost of their children's school education. Again the State provides us all with a free health service notwithstanding that the majority of the families in this country could well afford to pay for the medical care it requires, and that all but a very small proportion of the population could afford to pay the full prescription charges. What is more, the current demand on the resources of the health service by the population at large is unnecessarily large – which is not surprising. One does not need a training in economics to realize that people will want more of a good or service that is provided free than if, instead, they are charged the full cost of the resources required to provide it. That people 'over-use' the health service is the most common complaint of the doctors. This observation does not, however, exclude an economic argument for subsidizing particular medical services to most people, or even of providing all medical service free to particular groups of people. But no economic case has been established for providing all medical care free to everyone, rich and poor alike.

What, then, prevents the State from employing the selectivity principle in the distribution of the welfare services: in this instance, from redirecting a portion of the vast resources used in providing universal benefits away from those whose need of State aid in this form is small in order to increase the scale of benefits for the group forming the hard core of poverty in this country? The answer, strangely enough, is the opposition of many socialists and trade unionists. In accordance with the universalist principle there are socialists who insist on providing the rich with cash benefits whose value to them, the rich, are trifling in order that the really poor need not feel ashamed of accepting them also. In addition, there are the older members of the work force for whom the so-called Means Test cannot but evoke bitter memories of the inter-war period. Admittedly the Means Test was an unpleasant procedure by current standards of administration. But discrimination in the provision of benefits, either in money or kind, is transparently impossible without some means of ascertaining need. The resources are at hand and, in a rational community, the only issue would be that of devising a simpler, speedier, and more acceptable method of collecting the minimum information necessary to ensure that increased benefits, which can be made available in this way, are received by those most in need of them.

The facts and the arguments are familiar enough to economists who, in this instance, have often set out the alternative choices facing the community with commendable clarity.[1] But it is an uphill struggle. Such is the power of pride and prejudice in the modern world that the barrier to the most immediate and effective method of helping the needy to a decent standard of living – in effect wiping out the really degrading poverty that is totally unnecessary in a country as wealthy as Britain – is held in place by idealistic socialists and trade unionists, the very group in fact that should be in the forefront of any movement to bring about a redistribution of the national output in favour of the poor and the incapacitated.

III

(3) *Curbing Disamenity.* Leaving out the hard core of poverty in Britain, one should not expect any great accession of social welfare from attempts to accelerate the trend towards a more equal distribution of disposable income and wealth. In contrast, one may anticipate immediate and perceptible benefits from the introduction of legislation to call a halt to the chief sources of disamenity that afflict our daily lives.

Since Parts II and III are devoted to illustrating these particular afflictions we shall say no more about them here.[2]

[1] A recent and excellent discussion of the issues will be found in the December 1967 issue of *Encounter* by Arthur Seldon of the Institute of Economic Affairs.

[2] The inquisitive reader may be interested in some principles, familiar to economists, which will enable him occasionally to put a finer edge on the arguments.

We may take it for granted that the production of any good, whether for private or public enterprise, can be justified only on the principle that its value to society – as measured, in the first instance, by its full market value – exceeds its full cost of production. The principle further suggests that the output of any good being currently produced should be expanded so long as the market price

---

forthcoming for each successive unit exceeds the full increment of cost incurred in its production.

Now, if the output to be sold on the market is increased, the price per unit at which the lot can be sold will be lower (according to the 'law of demand'; which states that the lower a good is priced the larger the amount bought by the public). We may therefor infer that a social gain will continue to be made by expanding the output of any good – and, of course, necessarily reducing the price by as much as is necessary to sell the larger amount – until the price of the good in question only just covers, or is just equal to, its *increment* of cost; or, in the jargon, its 'marginal cost'.

This principle for determining the output of each good or service in the economy, by expanding it until price equals marginal cost, is commonly known as the 'marginal-cost pricing rule', and the output so determined as the 'optimal' output.

In an economy that was highly competitive in all sectors the outputs of each of the goods and services produced would be close to optimal in this sense.

Part II

Spillover: Affliction of the Affluent Society

Chapter 4

What are Spillover Effects?

One cannot justify talking of one situation as an *economic improvement* compared with another without reference to premises on which judgements of better or worse are to be based. In the West they have usually been of a libertarian character: nothing is good for society unless it is held to be good by the individuals who form that society. And while it is true that there are people who appear to be incompetent judges of their own interests, this is usually regarded as an argument for education rather than for paternalism. Nevertheless, since there is no providential method of determining the true interests of any persons which would command general assent, it would be impolitic at this stage of the argument to premise propositions about social welfare on anything other than each man's view of his own interest. Though aware then of its occasional falsehood, we follow, provisionally, the liberal convention of accepting each man's judgement of his own interest.

Now it is a well-known proposition in economics that the operations of firms, or the activities of ordinary persons, have a variety of effects on other firms or persons of which no account is taken by the former group of firms or people. But we must be careful to distinguish one important category of effects – let us call them *spillover effects* – from the familiar adjustment repercussions arising simply from the interdependence of all prices and quantities in any well-functioning market system. To illustrate this latter type of repercussion, consider a substantial increase in the public's demand for liquid milk. Within a short period we can expect an increase in milk sales notwithstanding some rise in the cost of milk. The rise in the cost of liquid milk will clearly act to raise the price of butter, so reducing butter sales, which will tend in its turn to increase the demand, and price, of margarine and other fats that are a substitute for butter. Furthermore, the prices of beef, leather, and other goods will be affected as the economic system adjusts itself to the initial increase in the demand for liquid milk.

The dairy farmers, however, ignore all such repercussions which must follow their attempt to increase the amount of liquid milk produced. And, indeed, so long as all the relevant data enter into the calculus, as they do in a well-functioning market, there is not the slightest advantage to the economy in their taking any notice of the repercussions that work their way through the whole system of prices and quantities. Every change in consumers' demand and every change in technology produce greater or lesser adjustments throughout the whole economy, adjustments that are warranted under a well-functioning and competitive market system.

In contrast, spillover effects are distinguished by their being, unwarrantably, left out of the calculus from the start. It happens innocently enough. Machines that are employed to produce services for the public may simultaneously produce 'disservices'. The recipients of the services acknowledge their value by a willingness to pay for them. Symmetrical reasoning would require that the recipients of disservices receive sums of money in compensation for the damage sustained. Things do not work out this neatly, however. If, say, in producing vacuum cleaners a manufacturer incidentally produces a great deal of smoke from his factory chimneys, proper social accounting would require him to determine the value not only of the 'good' produced (vacuum cleaners), but the value also of the 'bad' (the smoke damage). The value of the damage suffered by others constitutes a cost to society. Clearly, then, the value of his *joint* product – vacuum cleaners *plus* smoke damage – will be less than the value of the vacuum cleaners alone by the costs of the smoke damage inflicted on the public.

Once account is taken of such spillover effects the social value of his enterprise is seen to be reduced. If the manufacturer were compelled to pay for the damage he causes[1] – or, alternatively, to pay for the installa-

---

[1] This suggestion offers an alternative method to that of subtracting the costs of the incidental damage from the market value of the vacuum cleaners, namely, that of *adding* them to the existing *commercial* costs of production in order to obtain the 'true' or *social* costs of production. Either method of adjustment will do – though, obviously, we cannot admit both adjustments simultaneously. We shall, in the following pages, tend to favour the latter method of adjustment as being more direct in its application.

tion of anti-smoke devices – his profits would be smaller. Moreover, once he had to add these costs to his normal commercial costs, he would have to reduce his sales. For only by restricting further the number of vacuum cleaners offered for sale will their price rise high enough to cover the resulting rise in his unit costs.

II

Why is it that spillover effects have not been brought more forcibly to the attention of the public? There may be more than one reason, and it will be revealing to discuss the several that come to mind.

First, the response of the growth-minded business economist to the allegation of damaging effects is to counter with the assertion that there are also many favourable spillover effects produced by industry. A perfume factory might incidentally sweeten the air for miles around. Bees raised for honey may fertilize the fruit trees of neighbouring farms. The construction of a dam might well improve the fishing upstream. The value conferred on others by these beneficial spillover effects would then have to be added to the value of the manufactured product in order to obtain the true social value.[1]

But the extent of these beneficial spillover effects makes no difference whatsoever to the main argument. Whether or not the economy is properly adjusted to the incidence of favourable spillovers, it still follows

---

For the inquisitive reader, in particular, the marginal cost rule (mentioned in the last footnote to Chapter 3) can be amended *either* to *social* value equals marginal (commercial) cost *or*, more common perhaps, to market value equals *social* marginal cost.

With this latter formulation in mind we should say that whenever an industry causes damaging spillover effects its social marginal cost will exceed its direct commercial marginal cost. The revised rule requires, therefore, that its price be set higher than before. Sales fall off and, consequently, the optimal output will be smaller than before.

The exception to this result occurs if the smoke damage is, so to speak, an overhead and, therefore, does not vary at all with the output produced by the factory. In that case the manufacturer's profits will be reduced, but without there being any incentive for him to contract his output. If the damage caused is large enough his net profit after meeting all claims will be negative. In that case he will cease to produce vacuum cleaners, at least in that locality.

[1] Alternatively, the value of the incidental benefits conferred on others should be subtracted from the commercial costs to yield us the social costs.

By symmetrical reasoning, the optimal output for such industries – reached by expanding outputs until prices are equal to their corresponding social marginal costs – will exceed their (uncorrected) competitive outputs.

that adjustment to smaller outputs is required in those industries producing damaging spillovers.[1] The importance of the latter depends entirely on their own incidence and magnitude, quite irrespective of the incidence and magnitude of beneficial spillovers.

Secondly, the professional economist has concentrated largely on spillover effects within an inter-industry context. The favoured examples are those spillovers produced by one industry or firm that fall on another industry or firm. The reason for this bias may be historical. The originator of the idea, Alfred Marshall, confined himself to the beneficial effects conferred on a particular industry as a result of an additional firm entering the industry. In any case, these inter-firm spillover effects are easier to calculate than those suffered by the public at large, and schemes for adjustment of output are more feasible as between organized groups than as between an unorganized public and the industries in question.

Thirdly, the professional economist, until very recently at least, regarded these spillover effects as one among several factors – such as the varying degrees of monopoly in the production of goods, or the incidence of indirect taxation on the price of goods – that stood in the way of some kind of ideal working of the economy: he tended to look upon them more as an obstacle to facile theorizing than as an existing social menace. Familiarity with so simple a concept, and ritual footnote references to it, seem to have imparted a feeling that the matter was well under control. In consequence, many economists continued to ignore the events taking shape around them and to immerse themselves instead in the intellectual fascination of quasi-mathematical models of growth, and the theoretical problems involved in the general solutions of optimal systems.

Fourthly, there is the undoubted difficulty of measuring the damages suffered by the public at large. The smoky factory chimney is so handy a classroom example of spillovers on to the public simply because it appears to limit itself to the dirt spread within the locality. The additional costs of keeping one's person and clothes clean in the smoke-polluted area can easily be estimated and added, along with such costs for all the others, to the commercial costs of producing any increment of product. The costs of water-pollution by one or more factories is also amenable to measurement wherever the authorities have estimates of the damage

[1] Except in the unusual case that in the production of some good both positive and negative spillover effects are generated, in which case they cancel to some extent, leaving a net negative or a net positive effect to be adjusted for.

caused to other industries or to the public at large. But the major social afflictions such as industrial noise, dirt, stench, ugliness, urban sprawl, and other features that jar the nerves and impair the health are difficult to measure and to impute to a single source – which is, of course, no reason for treating them with resignation.

Not that the damage wrought by these things is, in any case, entirely ignored. Apart from letters of protest and occasional newspaper comment, magazines such as *Punch* and *The New Yorker*, which specialize in social satire, frequently depict with biting humour the dilemmas of automobilization and the frustration of the millions all trying simultaneously to find a quiet place in the sun. But this does not meet the problem since, if anything, this laughing at the follies of mankind serves to release social tension and to make bearable that which, in fact, ought not to be borne with. If the problem is to be tackled by society, the economist must persist in revealing the nature of the beast, and must seek circumstances under which meaningful magnitudes may be attributed to the larger spillover effects.

Finally, and perhaps most important of all, there are proponents of *laisser-faire* at large who urge that nothing need be done. Given enough time and, presumably, forbearance, it will eventually sort itself out.

Their argument, in effect, takes its rationale from that of the protection racket in those areas where the police are either inefficient or corrupt. By paying some agreed bribe to the criminal gang the potential victim is left unmolested – an arrangement that has the virtue of leaving both him and the gang better off than if, instead, he refused to pay up. Likewise with spillover effects. I might well be able to bribe my neighbour not to use his diesel saw on a Sunday afternoon. The owner of a plant that uses the waters of a stream to produce soft drinks might also attempt to bribe the owners of a soap-producing plant that would otherwise pour its effluent into the stream. Such arrangements, if carried through, can be properly regarded as economic improvements, in that all are made better off by such voluntary agreements than they were in the previous situation.

The *laisser-faire* economist will always oblige by recognizing a difficulty here which, however, he turns to his advantage. In the simple cases above it was at least practicable for the single victim to buy himself some relief from the nuisance or damage. It becomes less practicable as the number of victims increase. It may well be that the most each family, residing in the neighbourhood of an airport, would pay to induce the airport authorities to site the airport elsewhere would amount to a sum that is more than enough to compensate both the airport authorities for the anticipated loss in choosing the next-best site and the anticipated losses of estate developers and others. Indeed, the total sum that could be offered might be very much larger than any conceivable gain the airport authorities and others could hope to secure. But under existing institutions the initiative for bringing about such an arrangement is not available. Even if it were, the costs of estimating and ensuring a fair contribution from each of some several score thousand families would be prohibitive. In the event, then, such potential economic improvements do not take place.

But, then, says our *laisser-faire* friend, is it exactly how it should be! For the costs of estimating and securing a fair contribution from each of several thousand families, also the costs of negotiating with the airport authorities – call these *decision costs* for short – are not by any means bookkeeping costs, or imaginary costs; they are real costs. And since such real costs exceed the value of the benefit to the affected households from closing down the airport[1] there would be a clear economic loss made in securing, by this sort of agreement, the removal of the airport. If, on the other hand, decision costs were low enough compared with potential benefits – and the setting up of government machinery for just such purposes might lower decision costs substantially – the agreement would be concluded and an economic improvement effected. Thus a few hundred families in the neighbourhood of a noisy tool factory might be able, without too much trouble and expense, to agree to club together to compensate the factory management for losses incurred in eliminating the noise.

We might well disagree with the justice of this sort of arrangement, but we should have to agree that it effected an economic improvement. The factory management is at least no worse off, and we must presume that the erstwhile noise victims are better off or they would not continue their payments.

III

There are, none the less, three weighty objections to the *laisser-faire* solution.

[1] The value of this benefit is measured here by the maximum amount householders would have been willing to pay *less* what in fact they would have to pay in full compensation to airport authorities to site the airport elsewhere.

First, as will be made clear in the following chapter, the decision costs involved in reaching agreements to curb spillover effects are, under the existing dispensation, unnecessarily heavy. If this is the case then many potential economic improvements remain unrealized.

Secondly, most of the larger spillover effects affecting amenity and health fall on the poorer groups within society, those in fact who are least able to sustain a reduction in their welfare.

The third objection, hinted at above, is the manifest inequity of such a solution. Admittedly the damage inflicted on others in the cases of spillover is incidental rather than deliberate. Yet it is no less inequitable that in such cases the victims should be made either to suffer the full extent of the damage wrought upon their lives or else to limit that damage by paying some appropriate sum.[1] Worse, the method provides no incentive for those responsible for spillover effects to limit them in the first instance. Quite the contrary: since the bribe that can be extracted depends upon the extent of the nuisance or damage, there is everything to be gained by surreptitiously increasing it.

Must we, then, seek a wholly political solution? A report, presented in 1967 to the U S Department of Health, Education and Welfare, listing an encyclopaedic range of environmental ills, proposes, characteristically, a vast programme of federal expenditure to combat them. It proposes also the appointment of a council of ecological advisers to shape a national policy on environmental management. In view of the prodigious expenditures envisaged and the implied extension of bureaucratic controls, we shall explore in addition to such controls two alternative but related approaches to a comprehensive solution to the spillover problem: (1) the enactment of 'amenity rights', which is discussed in the next chapter; and (2) the extension to environmental areas of the concept of separate facilities, which is discussed in Chapter 7.

[1] Not all adverse spillovers are to be regarded as inequitable, however. An inevitable by-product of a world in which material values predominate and inordinate expectations are encouraged is a growth in dissatisfaction with one's estate and a persistent envy of others. Such envy whether of others' status, achievements, or property, does come under the definition of spillover effects. But the terms of the argument do not require us to sympathize with the victim of this universal vice to the extent of proposing he be compensated. A normative study of the contribution an economist can make to the social welfare is necessarily guided by the broad value judgements common to the community. The welfare economist cannot be a strict utilitarian.

Chapter 5

Property Rights and Amenity Rights

I

The competitive market has long been recognized by economists as an inexpensive mechanism for allocating goods and services with tolerable efficiency. Once it is observed that the production of 'bads', or noxious spillover effects, have begun, increasingly, to accompany the production of goods, one might be excused for talking about a serious failure of the market mechanism. In fact the failure is not to be attributed to the market itself, but to the legal framework within which it operates. In particular, we must remind ourselves that what constitutes a cost to commercial enterprise depends upon the existing law. If the law recognized slavery the costs of labour would be no greater than the costs involved in capturing a man and maintaining him thereafter at subsistence level.

How, then, can the law be altered so as to remove the existing inequities?

In so far as the activities of private industry are in question, the alteration required of the existing law is clear. For private industry, when it troubles at all to justify its existence to society, is prone to do so just on the grounds that the value of what it produces exceeds the costs it incurs – gains exceed losses, in short. But what *are* costs under the law and what *ought* to be counted as costs is just what is in issue. A great impetus would doubtless take place in the expansion of certain industries if they were allowed freely to appropriate, or freely to trespass upon, the land or property of others. Even where they were effectively bought off by the property-owning victims, the owners of these specially licensed industries would certainly become richer. And one could be sure if, after the elapse of some years, the Government sought to revoke this licence there would be a tremendous outcry followed by a determined campaign of opposition alleging that such arbitrary infringement of liberties would inevitably stifle progress, jeopardize employment and, of course, 'lose the country valuable export markets'.

Such an example, though admittedly far-fetched, is dinstinctly relevant. For private property in this country has been regarded as inviolate for centuries. Even if the Government, during a national emergency or in fulfilment of some radical piece of legislation, takes over the ownership of private property it is obliged to compensate the owners. It may well be alleged that in any instance the Government paid too little or too much. But it would not occur to a British Government merely to confiscate private property.

In extending this principle of compensation, largely on the grounds of equity, the law should explicitly recognize also the facts of allocation. Privacy, quiet, and clean air, are scarce goods, far scarcer than they were before the war and sure to become scarcer in the foreseeable future. There is no warrant, therefore, for allowing them to be treated as though they were free goods; as though they were so abudant that a bit more or a bit less made not the slightest difference to anyone. Indeed, if the world were so fashioned that clean air and quiet took on a physically identifiable form, and one that allowed it to be transferred as between people, we should be able to observe whether a man's quantum of the stuff had been appropriated, or damaged, and institute legal proceedings accordingly. The fact that the universe has not been so accommodating in this respect does not in any way detract from the principle of justice involved, or from the principle of economy regarding the allocation of scarce resources. One has but to imagine a country in which men were invested by law with property rights in privacy, quiet, and clean air – simple things, but for many indispensable to the enjoyment of the good life – to recognize that the extent of the compensatory payments that would perforce accompany the operation of industries, of motorized traffic and airlines, would constrain many of them to close down – or else to operate at levels far below those which would prevail in the absence of such legislation, until such time as industry and transport discovered inexpensive ways of controlling their own noxious by-products.

Thus, if the law were altered so that private airport authorities were compelled to fully compensate victims of aircraft noise it is more than possible – even though the decision costs would be very much lower than those which would have to be incurred by the victims under the present law – that most airports would be quite unable to cover such costs with their profits. They would be recognized as uneconomic and would have to close down.[1]

II

The consequence of recognizing such rights in one form or another, let us call them *amenity rights*, would be far-reaching. Such innovations as the invisible electronic bugging devices currently popular in the US among people eager to 'peep in' on other people's conversations could be legally prohibited in recognition of such rights.[2] The case against their use would rest simply on the fact that the users of such devices would be unable to compensate the victims, including all the potential victims, to continue living in a state of unease or anxiety. So humble an invention as the petrol-powered lawn-mower, and other petrol-driven garden implements would come also into conflict with such rights. The

---

[1] Recent calculations of the differences in the market value of houses, alike in all other relevant respects, at different distances from an airport, understate the loss suffered from aircraft noise for at least two reasons:

(1) They represent an estimate of the maximum loss that the house-owner in the noisier area is able and willing to bear in order to move out of the area, not the larger estimate of the minimum sum they would accept to put up with the inconvenience. Moreover, as alternative quiet zones become harder to find, this minimum acceptable sum grows relative to the maximum sum they are willing to pay to move. Even if there were several currently quiet areas into which a family might move without great expense or inconvenience the absence of an announced government plan of maintaining these areas free of aircraft noise over the future leaves open a risk that reduces the attraction of such areas.

(2) If the Government's existing policies continue and, therefore, noise-free inhabitable areas soon disappear, the increased level of noise throughout the country as a whole is accompanied by a narrowing of differentials between areas. To regard such consequent differentials as an index of disamenity is absurd. For it will reveal zero disamenity for any area as the whole country becomes subject to the same amount of aerial disturbance, no matter how great.

[2] According to *Life International* (13th June, 1966): 'As manufacturers leap-frog each other turning out ingenious new refinements, the components they sell have been getting smaller and more efficient. . . . So rapidly is the field developing that today's devices may be soon outmoded by systems using microcircuits so tiny that a transmitter made of them would be thinner and smaller than a postage stamp, and could be slipped undetected virtually anywhere. . . . How to safeguard individual rights in a world suddenly turned into a peep-hole and listening-post has become the toughest legal problem facing the US today.'

Whether the law could be made effective is, of course, a problem. To the extent it could not, one would have to recognize a loss of welfare arising directly from technological progress.

din produced by any one man is invariably heard by dozens of families who, of course, may be enthusiastic gardeners also. If they are all satisfied with the current situation or could come to agreement with one another, well and good. But once amenity rights were enacted, at least no man could be forced against his will to absorb these noxious by-products of the activity of others. Of course, compensation that would satisfy the victim (always assuming he tells the truth) may exceed what the offender could pay. In the circumstances, the enthusiast would have to make do with a hand lawn-mower until the manufacturer discovered means of effectively silencing the din. The manufactuer would, of course, have every incentive to do so, for under such legislation the degree of noise-elimination would be regarded as a factor in the measurement of technical efficiency. The commercial prospects of the product would then vary with the degree of noise-elimination achieved.

Admittedly there are difficulties whenever actual compensation payments have to be made, say, to thousands of families disturbed by aircraft noise. Yet once the principle of amenity rights is recognized in law, a rough estimate of the magnitude of compensation payments necessary to maintain the welfare of the number of families affected would be entered as a matter of course into the social cost calculus.[1] And unless these compensatory payments could also be somehow covered by the proceeds of the air service there would be no *prima facie* case for maintaining the air service. If, on the other hand, compensatory payments could be paid (and their payment costs the company less than any technical device that would effectively eliminate the noise) some method of compensation must be devised.

It is true that the courts, from time to time, have enunciated the doctrine that in the ordinary pursuit of industry a reasonable amount of inconvenience must be borne with. The one defect of this otherwise judicious doctrine lies in the clear implication that the costs of such inconvenience be borne by the victim. In a world where the inconveniences are becoming increasingly intolerable the legal recognition of amenity

[1] Like collective goods, most collective 'bads' (such as aircraft noise) would, under amenity legislation, apparently place each person affected in a monopoly position: such a person could ask what price he wished in order to surrender the amenity in question, and could do so without fear of some other person's consent being 'substituted' for his. But this situation is no different from that of, say, landowners whose consent is required in order to lay a railway line. Just as a body of law has evolved to determine just compensation for the surrender of rights of way, so will the courts discover ways of giving effect to citizen's rights under amenity legislation.

rights has the virtue of imposing an economic interpretation on the word reasonable, and therefore also on the word unreasonable, by transferring the cost of the inconvenience on to the shoulders of those who cause it. If, by actually compensating the victims (or by paying to eliminate the disamenity by the cheapest technical method available) an existing service cannot be continued, the inconvenience that was generated is deemed to be unreasonable. And since those who cause the inconvenience are now compelled to shoulder the increased costs associated with it there should be no trouble in convincing them that the inconvenience is unreasonable or persuading them to withdraw the activity in question.

Governments may continue to claim that, say, a certain airline service should be maintained even though it cannot cover its social costs under such new legislation for reasons connected with the defence of the realm or the national interest. But it would now have to think twice about such popular formulae, since it would be required to vindicate its claims about the high value to the nation of this particular service by paying a direct subsidy to the operators of the service, from the taxpayers' money, in order to cover the costs of fully compensating the victims.

III

What is of prior importance, however, is that the ethical and economic principles served by amenity rights be accepted by law in the first instance. Once accepted, it will not overtax the wit of man to devise over time the machinery necessary to implement the law. But there should be no mistake about it; such a law will have the most drastic effects on private enterprise which, for too long, has neglected the damage inflicted on society at large in producing its wares. For many decades now, private firms have, without giving it a thought, polluted the air we breathe, poisoned lakes and rivers with their effluence, and produced gadgets that have destroyed the quiet of millions of families, gadgets that range from motorized lawn-mowers and motor-cycles to transistors and private planes. What is being proposed therefore may be regarded as an *alteration of the legal framework within which private firms operate in order to direct their enterprise towards ends that accord more closely with the interests of modern society.*

More specifically, it would provide industry with the pecuniary incentive necessary to undertake prolonged research into methods of removing the potential and existing amenity-destroying features of so many of today's products and services.

The social advantage of enacting legislation embodying amenity rights is further reinforced by a consideration of the regressive nature of the chief spillover effects. The rich have legal protection of their property and have less need, at present, of protection from the disamenity created by others. The richer a man is the wider is his choice of neighbourhood. If the area he happens to choose appears to be sinking in the scale of amenity he can move, if at some inconvenience, to a quieter area. He can select a suitable town house, secluded perhaps, or made soundproof throughout, and spend his leisure and pleasure in the country or abroad, and at times of his own choosing. In contrast, the poorer a family the less opportunity it has for moving from its present locality. To all intents it is stuck in the area and must put up with whatever disamenity is inflicted upon it.

And generalizing from the experience of the last ten years or so, one may depend upon it that it will be the neighbourhoods of the working and lower middle classes that will suffer most from the increased construction of fly-overs and fly-unders and road-widening schemes that inevitably tend to concentrate the traffic and thicken the pollution. Thus the recognition of amenity rights would have favourable distributive effects on the welfare of society. It would promote not only a rise in the standards of environment generally from which all would benefit, it would raise them most for the lower income groups that have suffered more than any other group from unchecked 'development' since the war.

IV

Finally, in any practical appraisal of the range of consequences following such an innovation, one must be aware that the existence of decision costs in making new economic arrangements does build inertia into the *status quo*. As mentioned above, the existence of potential economic improvements – that is, new economic arrangements whose value to some exceeds the losses incurred by others, thereby enabling everyone affected to be made better off – does not imply that they will or should be realized. It is necessary also that the decision costs entailed in effecting the change be smaller than the value of the potential economic improvement. Such decision costs, to say nothing of the need for initiative, act as a cost barrier to many potential economic improvements irrespective of the state of the law concerning the responsibility for amenity damages (although, as indicated earlier, the decision-cost barrier is likely to be very much greater for the existing law than for one recognizing amenity rights).

None the less, if we restrict ourselves to the number of spillover activities with potential economic improvements that would, because of their associated decision costs, be excluded under *either* law, the *status quo* resulting from the existing law will be markedly different from that resulting from a law recognizing amenity rights. And since there is this marked difference, it goes without saying that the law should be chosen with an eye to the status to be perpetuated. Neither state is 'optimal', in the economist's sense, while such inertia persists. But since the 'suboptimal' states are quite different, we should certainly want to choose the less intolerable suboptimal state.

In sum, under the existing law, a proliferation of adverse spillover effects continues to take refuge behind the barrier of decision costs. Under the proposed law, it is amenity which is sheltered behind this barrier. Using words loosely: the magnitude of decisions costs implies that under the *status quo* there will be 'too much' spillover; under the proposed status, on the other hand, there will be 'too little'.

Over time, of course, changes in population, in tastes, and in technology, may reduce some of the decision costs and may raise the value of the potential economic improvements under either law (though the converse seems just as likely). And wherever this occurs, wherever the value of the potential economic gain of some mutual arrangement exceeds the decision costs, the new arrangement will be brought into effect and we shall get the 'right amount' of spillover and the 'right amount' of amenity – an optimal outcome in fact. But bearing in mind that spillovers are likely to grow rapidly over the future, and that many of them, such as the destruction of natural beauty and the poisoning of the earth's atmosphere, cause irrevocable damage, the interests of society, certainly of posterity, is better served by 'too little' spillover rather than 'too much'. And, since in practice we have to choose between them, our continued acceptance of the *status quo* (rather than amenity legislation) implies an acceptance of the 'too much' spillover option.

Chapter 6

Outright Prohibition of Spillover

The most effective, and least expensive, way of curbing the riot of spillover that has spread over the country since the war is the enactment of a charter of amenity rights for the citizen, all of which rights are capable of being strictly enforced by the courts. A significant feature of such amenity rights, as described, is the complete prohibition of any of several clearly defined disamenities in the absence of consent among all the parties affected. This qualification is to be noted. If, for example, the owner of a diesel saw can afford to bribe all the families within earshot of his sawing operations to consent to his use of the saw, at least during certain hours, then everyone is made better off than he would be under a complete noise-prohibition. Again, if a helicopter pilot, or motor-boat operator, could afford to bribe all potential plaintiffs not to invoke the law, each member of the group (including the pilot or operator) would be better off than if the ban against noise were enforced within the locality.

For those spillovers involving noise, visual disturbance, or invasion of privacy, a waiver of rights contingent upon the consent of all interested citizens is clearly an economic improvement. But there are other sorts of spillover effects for which such a consensus to waive the prohibition might not be accepted as a potential economic improvement. And this for at least two reasons. First, there may be insufficient information on the range of consequences arising from the spread of the spillover in question. A citizen who agrees to put up with a certain type of spillover effect in return for a bribe may do so in ignorance not only of the risks to which he exposes his person and his family but also in ignorance of the risks to which he exposes an unknown number of people or humanity at large. The unpleasantness he experiences surrounded by exhaust fumes may be only a fraction of the damage ultimately inflicted on society. Similar remarks are pertinent to other forms of air pollution, to effluents poured in river, stream and lake, to the discharge of oil on the high seas, to the use of chemical pesticides and, above all, to the present creation of radioactive elements by peacetime nuclear reactors.[1]

Secondly, there are spillover effects that are experienced not only by citizens alive today but by future generations as well. Some of those effects mentioned in the former category can be included also among this type of spillover.[2] Other outstanding examples are development-spillover and tourist-spillover both of which involve the virtually irrevocable destruction of woodland, coastline, lake districts and places of rare natural beauty and magnificence. In consequence not only is the present generation deprived. The keen pleasure and solace offered by such scenic beauty is denied to future generations also. In such cases the State, in its role of custodian of the future, is obliged to overrule the narrower interests of any group of private citizens.

Spillover effects of these two types may, then, be entirely prohibited notwithstanding any potential agreement to waive the prohibition by a

[1] 'A new "dimension" of hazard is given also by the fact that while man now can – and does – create radioactive elements, there is nothing he can do to reduce their radioactivity once he has created them. No chemical reaction, no physical interference, only the passage of time reduces the intensity of radiation once it has been set going. . . .

Wherever there is life, radioactive substances are absorbed into the biological cycle. Without hours of depositing [radioactive waste products created by nuclear reactors] in water, the great bulk of them can be found in living organisms. Plankton, algae, and many sea animals have the power of concentrating these substances by a factor of 1,000 and in some cases even a million. As one organism feeds on another, the radioactive materials climb up the ladder of life and find their way back to man. . . .

The point is that very serious hazards have already been created by the "peaceful uses of atomic energy", affecting not merely people alive today but all future generations, although so far nuclear energy is being used only on a statistically insignificant scale. The real development is yet to come, on a scale which few people are capable of imagining.' (E. F. Schumacher, 'Clean Air and Future Energy', *Des Voeux Memorial Lecture*, October 1967.)

[2] According to a *Newsweek* report (8th January, 1968), Professor L. C. Cole of Cornell University, in a paper delivered at the 134th Annual Meeting of the American Association for the Advancement of Science, asks whether man is not destroying the earth's natural supply of oxygen. He points out (i) that the increasing combustion of fossil fuels has greatly accelerated the formation of carbon dioxides in the atmosphere, and (ii) that, in the US alone, some one million acres of suburbanized forest and grassland each year lose their ability to regenerate the oxygen supply through photosynthesis.

group of private citizens acting on limited information and in the mistaken belief that they alone are the only interested parties. Alternatively, the amenity legislation may contain a clause requiring, in all cases of proposed waiver by consent, the consent also of the Government which, would, however, be withheld for all spillover effects coming within the range of the above two categories.

Chapter 7

Separate Facilities

I

Returning to those spillover effects outside the special two categories discussed in the preceding chapter, the waiver-by-consent clause should be maintained with a view to preserving the opportunities of effecting potential economic improvements that may arise from time to time over the future in response to technical innovations and changes of taste. The universal application of amenity rights, so qualified, is wider perhaps than it might appear at first. In particular, no provision need be made in those cases where different people are affected in opposite ways by any particular spillover effect. It may well be that some people do not object to the loud noises of engines operated by others: they may even revel in them. It may also be the case that some people have become so accustomed to a carbon-monoxide polluted atmosphere as to suffer nausea in the presence of fresh country air. And it is far from unlikely that the post-war period has produced groups of people so habituated to uninterrupted radio noise – their own or anyone else's – that it would positively unnerve them to remain long in quiet surroundings. Such people would invariably choose to live somewhere along a traffic-infested main road than in a quiet cul-de-sac, and to recreate themselves on a transistorized beach rather than on a quiet one. But whatever the facts in the case, and however one judges the character of such people, the waiver clause entailing compensatory payments to victims of disamenity, as an instrument of economic improvement, may be extended to encompass situations such as these in which the reactions of one group are the opposite of those of the other group.[1]

[1] If the initial situation was such that those who produced transistor noise

46

Although the principle involved in this version of amenity rights seems to be unassailable both on grounds of improved allocation and social equity there are obvious practical difficulties in measuring and in implementing compensatory payments, difficulties that increase rapidly with the numbers of people that benefit or suffer in varying degrees from the activity in question. In other words, the decisions costs associated with economic improvements escalate rapidly as the numbers affected increase. And though we have affirmed it to be a far better thing if the law is such that prohibitive decision costs serve to perpetuate 'too much' amenity in the economy than if instead the law served to perpetuate an economy in which spillovers spread uninhibitedly, we should yet wish to advance social welfare both by seeking ways of reducing decision costs or by other methods. One method suggests itself if we recognize that we need not restrict ourselves to arrangements *within* a given area. Rather than seek an economic improvement within a single area, we may instead provide separate areas, or *separate facilities*, for each of the conflicting groups. This alternative solution offers distinct advantages. The larger the proportion of a given population having opposite attitudes, or reactions, to the remaining members, the more practical is the separate facilities solution and the greater is the economic benefit compared with a compensated change covering the entire area or population.

If, for example, about half the people in a large area enjoy a transistorized beach and the other half detest it, it would be useless to try to reach a decision by voting, as this would result in a tie. If the law favoured quiet, the transistor enthusiasts might try bribing the anti-transistor groups for complete licence to play or, failing that, for some limited concessions. Certainly if the transistor fans were rich and the anti-transistor group poor, they might succeed in coming to some agreement. And in that case everyone will be as well off, or better off, than he would be if, instead, the complete prohibition remained in force.

However, the population as a whole would be still better off if the

---

were few in number and, on the average, poorer than the anti-noise group, they may be unable to bribe their way to making any exception to the initial prohibition. In that case the existing prohibition is optimal: there is no system of payments between the groups in exchange for some transistor noise that would make them all better off. If, on the other hand, the transistor-loving group were wealthy and many compared with the opposing group, the optimal outcome might be that in which the latter group has been fully compensated to permit the transistor enthusiasts to play at will.

transistor enthusiasts were now exonerated from making any compensatory payments and, in addition, were permitted to revel freely in a medley of transistor noises – which would be the case if separate provision were made for the anti-transistor group. In short, providing a separate permissive beach for the transistor fans raises their welfare compared with the previous shared solution, while a separate beach for the lovers of peace and quiet makes them no worse off than they were when exactly compensated for any transistor noise. Thus, a separate-facilities solution, in these circumstances, further increases welfare – improving the lot of the transistor fans without diminishing the satisfaction of the anti-transistor group – beyond that reached by what we have called an 'optimal' solution within a single area.

Existing and familiar instances of separate-facilities solutions to such problems include the provision of separate smoking and non-smoking compartments in railway carriages and, in some cinemas, smoking in the balcony but not in the stalls. Pavements for pedestrians, though in a very limited way, belong to that sort of solution. And one could well multiply instances by the simple process of imagining many distinct activities being forced to share a common site, as, indeed, sometimes happens; for instance, a single field to be shared between soccer and rugger enthusiasts, or a single club room in which some men prefer that ladies be invited while others cannot abide so disturbing an arrangement, or in which there is a struggle over the issue of serving liquor or not. In all such cases, wherever it is practicable, separate facilities increase social welfare beyond the level that can be reached by a 'common to all' optimum arrangement within a single area.

This economic argument is buttressed by two others:

(i) In a swiftly changing world, traditions have no time to take root. There is apt to be less agreement than hitherto on the constituents of the good life. It is altogether possible that many people today enjoy the sedentary mechanized life offered by today's sprawling metropolis, along with the fume and din and tawdry façades. If so, it would be politically much simpler to encourage the creation of separate areas than to reach agreement about some ideal form of civilized living.

(ii) Apart from political expediency, there are humanitarian arguments which reinforce the welfare analysis developed in my book. There are many people today – call them frail, eccentric, hypersensitive or neurotic, if you wish – who find particular features of modern society increasingly unbearable. For some it is the sense of isolation, for others it is the pressure of keeping up with the machine, for yet others it is the sense of futility and despair, the incessant traffic, or the spreading wilderness of concrete and steel. Our affluent and technically competent society at present offers them no escape – no alternatives other than, perhaps, wandering off to India in a mad moment to die slowly of drugs or disease or starvation; or feeding on tranquillizers; or repeatedly falling sick, or attempting suicide. A variety of separate and viable areas, within which seemingly persecutory features of the Machine Age were absent, and within which more benign features were incorporated, appears to be a feasible proposition whatever the state of the law and one which an affluent society ought to offer to its members.

II

It is of some interest in this connection to realize that if amenity rights could be enforced at law the ordinary working of the market would tend to establish separate facilities. If, for example, the majority of people dwelling within one area preferred quiet while the majority in another area preferred motoring to the extent of being quite willing themselves to put up with the accompanying noise, motoring would be far cheaper in, and therefore would be attracted to, the latter area. On the same principle, airlines would avoid areas where quiet was most appreciated and concentrate on routes over which compensatory payments were smallest. Even if within areas of any size opinions for and against any activity were widely dispersed the tendency to bring about separate facilities would continue to operate wherever the interests of one of the parties were highly organized as indeed are the motoring and airline interests. Promoters of motoring would find it profitable to purchase areas of a given size (compensating the anti-motoring inhabitants either for moving or for putting up with the row) in which motoring enthusiasts could pursue their pastime unobstructed by speed limits and dwell together in roaring harmony.

Notwithstanding the operation of such a tendency in a community in which amenity rights were enforceable, there is no reason why the State should not, in addition to other measures designed to promote social welfare, take the initiative itself in providing separate facilities in order that the wants of those for whom quiet, clean air, and pleasant environment, were highly valued could be met without prejudice to those who 'couldn't care less'. Even if it transpired, which I very much doubt, that people who value such things are a small minority, the principle of amenity rights still warrants the creation of separate facilities for their enjoyment.[1]

Indeed, now that science has succeeded in launching humanity into the supersonic era it is of the utmost urgency that governments be prevailed upon to set aside large areas free of all aerial disturbance. The longer the delay the greater becomes the apparant dependence of economy upon such flights; the more are industrial operations re-scheduled to the new speeds, the further the process of integrating supersonic flights with the existing system of transport, and the more massive the build-up of vested interests. If reservations were set aside in the United States as a matter of justice for the American Indians who wanted no part of the society of the white man, a similar justice is due to citizens who wish to opt out of the supersonic society. Certainly it would be an act of manifest injustice forcibly to subject noise-sensitive citizens to arbitrary and continual noise bombardment. But this is unavoidable in the absence of noise-free zones. Such zones are in any case prerequisite to experiment with a variety of separate areas offering wider choice to people in respect of environmental quality. And it is perhaps unnecessary to add at this stage of the argument that if, in so small a country as Britain, the reservation of large viable zones, conveniently placed yet free from aerial disturbance, were technically impossible then supersonic flights over the country would almost certainly be economically impossible under any effective system of amenity legislation. For once amenity rights were enacted specifically to protect the citizen against such molestations, the sums required to compensate fully the millions of potential victims would be sure to exceed the most optimistic estimates of the profits that could be made by operating supersonic flights within the country.

In the meantime regional authorities could make a start by setting aside large residential areas through which no motorized traffic is per-

[1] One of the oft-alleged virtues of the price system, in comparison with the system of decisions based on majority voting, is that a properly functioning price system is responsive to minority tastes. Even in the context in which this generalization is commonly understood, its truth depends largely upon the organization of the market and the existing technology. Nevertheless, once a stage is reached in economic development beyond which the generation of external diseconomies competes with the generation of the national product, the wants of minorities – and even those of majorities – are increasingly ignored by the private enterprise price system. Only political power is then able to redress this social evil either through government intervention, direct and indirect, and/or through legislation establishing rights of amenity.

mitted to pass and over which no aircraft is permitted to fly, and by prohibiting motor-boats on the lakes in certain districts and traffic in general from the choicer bits of National Trust property. Municipalities also have an important role to play in keeping motor traffic from certain shopping areas, from narrow roads, from cathedral precincts, and from other places of beauty and historic interest that can be enjoyed only in a quiet traffic-free setting.

And surely such proposals seem reasonable enough in themselves without labouring their economic rationale. After all, there is already too much of a muchness; every road crawling with automobiles, the air of every town and village fouled with their gas, to be relished by all who have stomach enough for these things. No enthusiastic 'pace-maker' need feel himself deprived if some areas in Britain are set aside for the quiet-loving minority – if it is a minority. Nor should all such areas display the same features; there is room enough for a wide range of social experiment in living together. One need have no objection what-soever to developing areas specifically for the enthusiastic motor-cyclists, for the 'young in heart' and for the would-be young, over which they could ride around for hours without unavoidably annoying those whose tastes run to other things. At the other extreme, decent residential areas could be set aside for those 'backward-looking' people who would be glad to abolish the use of all engines outside the home and for eccentrics who would prefer to dwell in areas admitting only horses and horse-drawn vehicles as means of transport. If they are prepared to pay for it – and there is no reason why any such arrangement should cost more to operate, rather than less, compared with existing modern arrangements – there is no advantage to the rest of the country in depriving them of their wants.[1] In between, there should be a wide variety, some areas having no more than large pedestrian precincts, or traffic-free shopping islands, to distinguish them, others permitting only public transport or electrically-powered transport on their roads, others yet prohibiting all types of motorized vehicles, or prohibiting them between certain hours, and many of them refusing airline compensation in order to remain free from aerial disturbance.[2]

[1] All such relatively 'primitive' areas would presumably be connected with the rest of the country by rail, though of course the wishes of the inhabitants would be taken into consideration.

[2] There should be no great difficulty in determining the right size and number of any particular type of separate facility. Larger numbers of people per square yard, or square mile, congregating in type A facility compared with

With almost all the convenient and desirable areas close to the metropolis, and with many other desirable towns and villages already shaped for a motorized society, heavy capital costs may have to be incurred in 'reconverting' suitable places to amenity areas. In conformity with the principles laid down in this and previous chapters, however, if the value to inhabitants of any such potential amenity area – estimated as the minimum sum required to compensate them in forgoing their legal rights to amenity – exceeds the capital costs of converting the area, social welfare and equity is advanced in creating such an area.

III

Business economists have ever been glib in equating economic growth with an expansion of the range of choices facing the individual; they have failed to observe that as the carpet of 'increased choice' is being unrolled before us by the foot, it is simultaneously being rolled up behind us by the yard. We are compelled willy-nilly to move into the future that commerce and technology fashions for us without appeal and without redress. In all that contributes in trivial ways to his ultimate satisfaction, the things at which modern business excels, new models of cars and transistors, prepared foodstuffs and plastic *objets d'art*, electric tooth-brushes and an increasing range of push-button gadgets, man has ample choice. In all that destroys his enjoyment of life, he has none. The environment about him can grow ugly, his ears assailed with impunity, and smoke and foul gases exhaled over his person. He may be in circumstances that he will never enjoy a night's rest at home without planes shrieking overhead. Whether he is indifferent to such an invasion of his privacy, whether he suffers it stoically or painfully, whether he is resigned or furious, there is under the present dispensation practically nothing he can do about it.

Under the circumstances, then, the popular cliche, 'the costs of progress' misconstrues the issue. For it suggests a *quid pro quo*, a

---

type B might be taken as an index of the increased popularity of type A compared with B, and steps taken to increase the size and/or number of them until some equilibrium were established. In comparing different types of residential areas, however, there should be no objection to guidance by market forces. Once the range of alternative areas has been sufficiently increased, the relative size and number of, say, type C and type D areas may be determined by the demand for them. All that is required is imagination in the design of such areas and initiative in their provision.

voluntary surrender of certain conveniences in exchange for the manifest benefits vouchsafed to us by industrial progress. If, indeed, each one of us agreed to accept the incidence of 'bads' (the adverse spillovers) in order to have the opportunity of buying the additional goods and services put on the market, the 'costs of progress' response could be rationalized. But since there is, in fact, no economic mechanism which offers to each of us this over-all choice, the phrase must be repudiated. True one person may attach quite different weights to the 'bads' and the 'goods' compared with another person. Not every reader can be expected to share my distate for much of the stuff produced by modern industry. But whatever one's personal evaluation of the terms of exchange, the fact that the terms of exchange are imposed upon a man cannot be gainsaid. The 'bads' are not chosen by him: they are forced upon him. And this form of coercion affronts, or should affront, the liberal conscience.[1]

To conclude, extension of choice in respect of environment is the one really significant contribution to social welfare that is immediately feasible. As suggested, however, it is not likely to be brought about by market forces working within the existing legal framework. Legal recognition of amenity rights, on the other hand, would touch off government and private initiative in creating a wide diversity of residential environments offering to all men those vital choices that have too long been denied them.

---

[1] Indeed, the liberal's justification, if not his commendation, of a good pricing system is based on the belief that it is an instrument of personal freedom. It enables people to choose among individual goods – and at supply prices which reflect their real resource cost. If 'bads' (i.e. adverse spillover effects) are also produced, symmetrical reasoning would require a pricing system which allows people to choose which 'bads', and how much of each, to take at the going price – which supply price itself should reflect the excess gain of the producer of incidental 'bads'. If, however, the economic system is such that a growing range of 'bads' are being *forced* on to people, there can be no presumption that on balance the area of choice is expanding.

Part III

The Magnitude of the Affliction

Chapter 8

Dereliction of the City:
Overcrowding and Uglification

I

The advantages of the city are too obvious to dwell upon. Regarded as a commercial centre it may attract buyers and sellers from all over the country by offering a wide range of specialized services. In the past the city was the centre also of intellectual, artistic and scientific achievement. And today only the city, the big city or metropolis, can provide a sophisticated public large enough to form daily audiences for symphony orchestras, operas, ballets and theatres. Returning to more mundane matters, the scale of operation of such public services as water, gas, electricity, and even administration, may show appreciable economies. There are, however, technological limits to the economies of size, and if such economies were the sole consideration, we might want to promote the expansion of the city until they were all fully exploited – until, that is, it was no longer possible to lower the marginal cost of any good or service by increasing the size of the city, measured either by area, population density, or wealth.

But even assuming these economies of size to be large, there are countervailing diseconomies of size. The larger the city the more time and resources have to be spent within the city on the movement of people and goods. Even telephone communication can become wasteful as the numbers in commerce and the professions increase. Any growth of building densities in city centres adds further to the difficulties of traffic that has passed the point of mutual frustration.

It might be thought that in some providential manner all this 'comes out in the wash', the right size being determined by a balance of forces in which the increasing economies are offset by increasing diseconomies.

But whatever the equilibrium of forces, it is hardly one that providentially issues in a city of optimal size. There is, in fact, an asymmetry in the forces at work which tends to make the city too large. The economies of large-scale productions are apparent and there is every incentive for their exploitation by private and public companies.[1] Indeed, the more obvious economies of a metropolitan area such as London – local availability of skilled labour and specialized personnel, accessibility to market and technical information, the provision of finance and other facilities – are so widely recognized as in fact to be overrated.[2] Even if we assumed a complete absence of countervailing forces, the scope for further exploitation of the economies of scale are likely to be negligible.[3] On the other hand, the effects of any additional population, in adding to the traffic, and ultimately in time spent commuting, in adding to the noise and grime, also the impact of this increased pressure on people's health and disposition are not taken into account by commerce and industry. Important though they are, they are difficult to measure. In the absence of pertinent legislation the incentive for expanding firms to bring them into the cost calculus is virtually non-existent.

II

The extent of the social damage inflicted by traffic congestion, even on itself alone, tends to be underrated by a public which habitually thinks in terms of an average figure rather than in terms of the appropriate marginal concept. A homely example illustrates the point. Three men can sit comfortably on one side of the seats of a corridor train operated by

[1] An 'optimal exploitation' takes place, however, only if the companies act as discriminating monopolists, or are guided by marginal-cost pricing.

[2] Despite the assumption of *laisser-faire* economists that businessmen know their own interests best, there is ample evidence to show that many private firms have an *irrational* (non-commercial) preference for expanding within the metropolis rather than for setting up branches in other regions of the country. In particular, see the evidence put forward in a paper by Dr Needleman, 'What are we to do about the Regional Problem?' *Lloyds Bank Review*, January 1965.

[3] Bear in mind also that the larger the economies of scale realized the more widespread are the effects of any accidental breakdown of public utilities, in the public transport system, the electricity supply, the telephone service or water supply. How vulnerable a large metropolis can be to a withdrawal of essential services for even a short period of time has recently been examplified by the electricity failure (1965) and transport strike (1966) in the New York area.

British Rail. The addition of one man will generally result in all four sitting a little too close for comfort. The additional man, in reaching a decision, need only weigh the advantage to himself of standing as against the alternative of sitting wedged between two others. He need take no account whatsoever of the increased discomfort of the other three if he decides to sit down.[1] The same principle is at work on the roads. Suppose that each hour no more than about one thousand cars can drive comfortably down a given stretch of road. Each additional car contemplating the use of the road need reckon only the incipient congestion it has itself to put up with. If we ignore all other social costs and assume, for argument's sake, that the increment of cost caused by the additional motorist is about the same as that suffered also by each of the existing one thousand, then the total of these increments of cost suffered by all is about one thousand times as great as that experienced by the additional motorist. None the less, this additional motorist makes a decision whether or not to use the stretch of road in question by reference only to his own increment of cost – one thousandth part of total increment of cost.

An unregulated traffic flow, therefore, tends to be too large. By one means or another it should be reduced to an 'optimal' traffic flow; one at which the total marginal, or incremental, cost of congestion is no greater than, and if possible equal to, the value placed on driving in the stream of traffic, bearing in mind the price of the alternative modes of travel.

The same principle applies to the additional firm that settles in a crowded city, so adding personnel and traffic that further impede the movement of others in the city. The firm, however, need take account only of its relatively negligible share of the additional inconvenience it inflicts on everyone. Analogous remarks apply to constructing additional floor space, and to demolishing an old building in order to build a taller one with a more 'economical' use of floor space. They need take no account of the spillover effects on the city's traffic.

---

[1] The question of whether or not the train must travel packed in this way in order to make a profit is irrelevant to the principle at issue, which is simply that of the full additional cost of the fourth man's taking a seat. If he were compelled to take into consideration the inconvenience borne by each of the others on taking a seat by a rule requiring his compensating each one of them, he might well make a decision to stand all the way rather than sit. The principle holds also irrespective of the method for determining which of the four shall be faced with the decision.

Of no less topical interest is the growth of the city's population. Each person who chooses to live in the metropolis has no thought of the additional costs he necessarily imposes on others, and especially over the short period during which it is not possible to add to the existing accommodation,[1] road space or public transport facilities. In the more crowded parts of the metropolitan area it requires no more than a few thousand immigrants to reduce in remarkable degree the standard of comfort of all the previous inhabitants of the area. If the immigrants into the city happen to arrive from others parts of the country, or from others parts of the world enjoying comparable standards, the degree of discomfort suffered by the existing inhabitants, though incompatible with any optimal situation, will remain within limits. For such immigration will not continue if living conditions in such areas fall too far below the standards generally expected. If, on the other hand, immigrants come from countries with standards of living, of hygiene and comfort, well below those prevalent in the host country, the standards of the neighbourhood within which the immigrants elect to settle may have to decline drastically before the standards themselves begin to act as a disincentive to further immigration. Indeed, the immigrants may be willing to tolerate worse conditions than in the homeland since (i) those who pioneer the immigration will be prepared to endure hardship for a year or two in the hope of bettering their lot later; and (ii) some are resigned to dwell in squalid conditions for several years with the aim, initially at least, of amassing a sum of money in order either to return or to bring over their families. Moreover, there is always a time-lag, measured perhaps in years, between the worsening of conditions in immigrant areas of the city and the general appreciation of this fact in the immigrants' homelands.

III

Spillover effects, favourable and adverse, have relevance also to the physical layout of the city. A building in the city today is seldom regarded by the owners as more than a financial asset. But it may, in addition, be an asset or liability to the other citizens. A stately building

[1] In the absence of a rise in economic rents (which would distribute the limited accommodation so as to realize an optimal situation) the additional newcomer imposes inconveniences on others in excess of his payments to the landlord.

is a source of pleasure and pride to the citizens, while a shoddy building, of which there has been a proliferation since the war, is a source of annoyance and disgust. If the builder of these 'functional' modern steel and glass blocks were compelled to compensate citizens for 'uglifying' their city, we might yet have hope for the future. When one considers that the architecture of the city influences the humour and character of its citizens; when one considers the civic pride and sense of community that may be inspired by the architecture of a city, it is a telling reflection on our kind of civilization that we leave the initiative in designing our cities, piecemeal, largely to commercial interests, and the approval thereof to close-fisted councillors.

Imagine, then, an alternative dispensation in which some sort of ideal city is established having wide boulevards, majestic buildings, and spacious parks. The site of the city, we suppose, is owned entirely by an enlightened muncipality which, as a matter of course, sets up a select committee of citizens, each renowned for his taste and judgement, charged with promoting the beauty and dignity of the city.[1] If the committee become convinced of the virtues of the price mechanism to the point of willingness to sell land for development by private companies it could none the less ensure the working of 'the invisible hand', provided it sold only on condition that purchasers defrayed all relevant social costs. These would be defined to include sums of money fixed by the committee as adequate compensation to citizens who continually would have to bear unsightly or incongruent edifices plus sums to compensate for additional disamenities such as increased traffic and air pollution. Extending the market under these conditions may be expected to provide incentives to preserve and promote the beauty of the city – at least, if it did not do so, the fault could be laid squarely on the shoulders of the citizenry. Whatever the outcome one must admit the possibility of problems arising in estimating adequate compensation. But the problems arise as an inevitable result of facing the issue squarely, of attempting to bring into the calculus those social costs that are, under

[1]The principles by which local authorities and, ultimately, the central government, exercise limited control on building do not correspond with those proposed here. Local officers see themselves primarily as watchdogs of the 'public interest' guided by an *ad hoc* set of criteria. They are peculiarly vulnerable to accusations of 'holding up' progress, or discouraging growth and employment, and they can seldom resist the argument that 'development' will bring in increased revenues.

existing institutions, systematically ignored to the undeniable detriment of our towns and cities.[1]

In view of the rampant post-war development not only in London and other cities but also in innumerable seaside resorts and small towns of Britain, which before the war had still some remnants of local character, there is a particular urgency in recognizing these social costs. Intimate local architecture is everywhere being swamped by anonymous concrete egg-crates and the 'new' slab architecture equally suitable and equally monotonous in London, Berlin, Buenos Aires and Singapore.[2]

[1] A more conservative version of this scheme, and one that does not require any institutional alteration, would seem to be to arrange for a committee of citizens to bid against the private builder in an open market. However, as we have seen, the results would not in general be the same. The maximum amount that the citizens would be willing to pay for land in order to bid it away from private use would be less than the minimum the citizens would be prepared to accept if they already owned the land. One would want to favour the method proposed in the text, however, not only for distributional reasons but also in support of the principle of vesting amenity rights in the citizens.

[2] I am far from suggesting that the architect be given a free hand, though his opinions are worth hearing and would become more so were he under less pressure to seek new forms and new methods of using materials, just because they are not traditional. To a great number of people traditional materials and older styles afford far more pleasure than the modern buildings that accord with a trend towards unadorned functionalism. We still find delight in many examples of Georgian or Regency architecture. The Crescent at Regent's Park, St Paul's Cathedral, Somerset House, are justly prized not only because of their historic associations but for their inherent beauty and humanity. Much of this eighteenth and early nineteenth century architecture is suggestive of the better features of those times, of spaciousness, proportion, leisure and splendour. It is with a sense of relief that the eye picks them out from the dreary uniformity of most modern city blocks. Certainly if we cannot do better than the present assortment of engineering monstrosities – from which, for monumental folly, the palm must be handed to the architects of the Elephant and Castle centre – we had best call a halt to further building. Indeed, if we were emancipated enough to ignore strong religious feelings about 'progress', and to recognize that the new was the enemy of the excellent, a good case could be made for a programme of removing the post-war crop of eye-sores, and replacing them by an older and more intimate style of architecture.

Chapter 9

Dereliction of the City:
Traffic Congestion

I

Let us pause at this juncture to contemplate modern society's greatest nightmare, motorized traffic. The city as a centre point of civilization, as a place of human concourse and life and gaiety is becoming a thing of the past. Hoarse beneath the fumes emitted by an endless swarm of crawling vehicles, today's city bears closer resemblance to some gigantic and clamorous arsenal. None of the present piecemeal attacks on the sorest affliction of twentieth-century society have led to any noticeable improvement. The transport economist's solution does not take one very far. One can estimate 'marginal congestion costs' and infer some 'optimal' traffic flow which, as suggested in Appendix C, need not be very different from the existing flow – but only by ignoring, often explicitly, the so-called intangibles that can be by far the more important part of the diseconomies inflicted by traffic on the city. The same blind eye is in evidence when estimating 'optimal' parking charges or the rate of return on roadbuilding, and when wielding the now fashionable technique of cost-benefit analysis. Sometimes, as a gesture of technical bravado, economists may add to the social cost of motorized traffic an estimate of the costs to the community of the number of fatal accidents by the felicitous device of reckoning the cost of a man killed as the loss of his potential future pecuniary contribution to the national product. At any rate, it is a device that has the virtue of keeping the cost low to the motoring community as the trend continues towards an increasing proportion of aged people in the total kill. Many of the aged, of course, contribute practically nothing to the national product and, on this principle therefore, their loss to the nation is negligible.[1]

The piecemeal methods of engineers in the face of traffic problems differ only from those of the economist in being cruder. They turn on the location of 'growing points' in the traffic, and on a variety of formulae, based on traffic growth relative to road capacity, that yield critical ratios purporting to justify increased investment. These formulae are supplemented by *ad hoc* decisions on building bridges, circuses, by-passes, diversions, fly-overs and fly-unders, whenever something 'has to be done'. If the engineers could save us by such methods, or by even more grandiose ones, we should by now have had ample evidence of their success in the United States where, in many cities, muncipal engineers have been bending over backwards for years in the endeavour to accommodate the motorist. Yet no relief is in sight. Far from it, cities like New York, Detroit, Los Angeles, lie prostrate beneath an army of mechanized locusts that have devoured them heart and soul.

The over-all response of governments since the war has been to do little more than to make stern noises about efficiency while allowing, nay encouraging, the use of the nation's limited resources to install more plant to produce more cars, lorries, and scooters, that show a profit to their makers, and a gain to their users, by steadfastly ignoring the mounting costs of traffic control, of mutual frustration, and of the barely tolerable pressure of noise, stench, dirt and exasperation, to say nothing of the increasing figures for death and mutilation. For the popular journalist, impatient of tomorrow's cornucopia of gadgets, the accumulation of disamenities and the vexations of modern living may be dismissed as the 'inevitable costs of progress'. But to the economist they

---

[1] An unqualified rejection of this principle has been made in an early paper by Professor Eli Devons, 'The Language of Economic Statistics', reprinted in *Essays in Economics* (1961).

A more meaningful economic measure of the cost of accidents would be the compensation necessary to induce each individual in the community to accept the risks associated with motoring *under present conditions*. Some, of course, would be glad to stick their necks out for nothing. At the other extreme would be those who could hardly be bribed by any price if there were any choice in the matter. At this other extreme we might have to answer the question: how much should the motor-enthusiast have to pay the potential corpse for depriving him of life and liberty? There is more than one way of reckoning the social costs of a pastime that has the incidental effect of killing off one's fellows. And reckoning it the hard way – at unimaginably large sums necessary to satisfy those who want to be no part of the motorized society – seems right to me, even if it would entail the abolition of private motoring in any collective choice.

constitute a growing tangle of spillover effects that, partly by their nature but more by historical accident, have escaped the pricing mechanism.

So far only one radical proposal appears to have been put forward by the engineers to meet the road problem, that in the famous report by Professor Colin Buchanan who was asked in 1962 by Mr Marples, the then Minister of Transport, to 'study the long-term development of roads and traffic in urban areas and their influence on urban environment'. Buchanan became convinced of one thing: that present developments could not be allowed to continue. Unless something was done soon, he warned the public, the usefulness of vehicles in towns would decline rapidly, and pleasantness and safety would 'deteriorate catastrophically'. He rejected the Government's then existing policy of small-scale road improvements designed to keep the traffic moving at all costs as being self-defeating. Such 'improvements' would, he prophesied, be overtaken by the increase in traffic as soon as they were finished.[1] Yet, notwithstanding his graphic descriptions of the damage and disamenity wrought on our lives by the private automobile, he based his recommendations on premises similar to those furnished in the Report's introduction by Sir Geoffrey Crowther: that the motor-car was 'a potentially highly beneficial invention' and its future was assured. There were $10\frac{1}{2}$ million vehicles in 1962. By 1970 we could expect this number to increase to 18 million. By 1980 there should be some 27 million vehicles on our roads, growing to about 40 million by the end of the century. Apparently it would be futile to fight against this trend as it appeared that the population was as intent on owning cars as were the manufacturers in providing them.

Starting from such 'modernistic' propositions it is not surprising that Buchanan goes on to argue that if the present-day town is unsuitable for the motor-car then it must be rebuilt so that we can have the traffic we want along with the amenity we also seek. Having established a need for his expertise he proceeds to consider the various principles of road construction such as the corridor system which would set up 'environmental areas' within an interlacing network of highways. In particular

[1] A 'Parkinson's Law' for traffic: that private motoring expands so as to fill the road space made available, is readily explained by the existing motoring potential and its growth relative to the physical constraints. At the time of writing, for instance, of the total number of private car-owners in the London area only an estimated 7 per cent use them for commuting into central London.

he lays stress on the need for 'traffic architecture' which involves an integration of buildings and roads at different levels.

But before succumbing to the futuristic visions of benevolent technocrats, the economist should pause to consider the full social costs of their attempted implementation in this already overpacked island of ours, costs that are better appreciated by comparing Buchanan's proposals not with the existing chaos – which would, admittedly, render it attractive – but rather with other radical alternatives. For even if the social costs of the existing situation, of the Buchanan Plan and of the alternatives to it are not easily measurable, the public's range of choice is broadened by revealing to it technologically feasible opportunities hitherto unconsidered. In the particular case of transport, with its pervasive repercussions on our ways of living, such alternatives must necessarily include schemes of resource-allocation other than those presented to us either by the existing market mechanisms, modified by a patchwork of government regulations, or by the humane aspirations of engineers.

II

The social significance of both the market and the engineering criteria involved, as well as that of the alternative solution proposed here, may be better understood if, for a while, we skirt direct controversy and approach these issues by a sort of parable. Thus, without straining his creduility perhaps, the reader may be able to picture to himself a region of some continent, say, on the other side of the Atlantic, in which the traditional right to carry firearms is never questioned. Indeed, on the initiative of the manufacturers, who spend colossal sums in advertising their new wares, more than one pistol is to be seen in a man's belt. The young men in particular are anxious to be seen with the latest de-luxe 'extra hard-hitting' model. Obviously the manufacture of holsters and other accessories flourishes as also does the manufacture of bullet-proof vests, leggings and helmets. These are not the only growth industries, however, for notwithstanding the purchase of bullet-proof items, the members of the undertakers association do a flourishing trade. The windows of all but the poorer houses are fitted with shatter-proof glass, while the bullet-proofing of rooms and offices in the more dangerous districts is a matter of ordinary precaution. No family is foolish enough to neglect the training of their sons, and even their daughters, in the art of the quick draw. In any case, a number of hours each week is devoted to target practice and dodgery in all the best schools. Life insurance is, of course, big business despite the exorbitant premia, and expenditure on medical attention continues to soar. For in addition to such normal ailments, as bullets embedded in various parts of the anatomy, there is widespread suffering from a variety of chafed skin diseases, the result of wearing the unavoidably heavy bullet-proof apparel. Moreover, owing to nervous diseases and anxiety, about every other adult is addicted either to strong liquor or to tranquillizing drugs. Taxes are burdensome for obvious reasons: a swollen police force employed mainly in trying to keep down the number of victims of the perennial feuds, extensive prisons and prison hospitals, to say nothing of the public funds devoted to guarding offices, banks, schools, and to the construction of special vans for transporting the children to and from schools.

In such an environment the most peace-loving man would be foolish to venture abroad unarmed. And since it is observed by the *laisser-faire* economist that men freely choose to buy guns, it would be regarded as an infringement of liberty to attempt to curb their manufacture. Moreover, since the market is working smoothly, the supply of firearms being such that no one need wait if he is able to pay the market price, no government intervention to match industrial supplies to rising demand is called for. Provided there is enough competition in the production of firearms so that over the long period prices just cover costs (and tend also to equal marginal costs of production) the allocation economist is well satisfied. Looking at the promising signs of growth in the chief industries, firearms and accessories, the business economist pronounces the economy 'sound'. If, however, for any reason the Government begins to have misgivings about some of the more blatant social repercussions, it consults with the pistol economist, a highly paid and highly regarded expert. The pistol economist constructs models and, with the help of high-powered statisticians, amasses pistological data of all kinds, from which he calculates the optimal set of taxes on the sale of pistols and ammunition in recognition of those external diseconomies, such as occasional corpse-congestion on the better streets whose monetary costs can, he believes, be estimated.

Notwithstanding all his scientific advice, matters eventually come to a head, and amid much government fanfare a committee of inquiry is set up under the chairmanship of a highly competent engineer, Mr B. If there ever was a realist, Mr B. is one, and he soon satisfies himself that

the economy is heavily dependent upon pistol production and all the
auxiliary industries and services connected therewith. Besides, the
evidence is incontrovertible: the demand for guns continues to grow
year by year. It must, therefore, be accepted as a datum. Undaunted,
Mr B. faces 'the challenge' by proposing a radical remodelling of the
chief towns and cities, at an unmentionable cost, in the endeavour to
create an environment in which people can have both their guns and a
peaceful life as well. The chief features of his plan are based on what he
aptly calls 'pistol architecture', and includes provision for no-shooting
precincts fenced high with steel, the construction of circular and wavy
road design to increase the difficulties of gun-duelling, the erection of
high shatter-proof glass screens running down the centres of roads to
prevent effective cross-firing, and the setting up of heavily protected
television cameras at all strategic positions in the towns in order to relay
information twenty-four hours a day to a vast new centralized police
force equipped with fleets of helicopters. Every progressive journalist
pays tribute to the foresight and realism of the B-plan and makes much
of the virtues of 'pistol architecture', the architecture of the future. Alas,
the Government begins to realize that any attempt to raise the taxes
necessary to implement the B-plan would start a revolution. So the plan
is quietly shelved, new committees of inquiry are formed, masses of
agenda are produced, and things continue much as before.

III

We need not continue save to press home a few parallels. Over the last
fifty years we have witnessed a transposition of ends and means.
Originally the motor vehicle was designed for the roads. Today roads are
designed for vehicles. Originally the motor vehicle was to be fitted into
the pace of life. Today the pace of life is adapted to the speed of the
vehicle, the saddest casualty of all being an irretrievable loss of the
sense of ease, space and leisure.

   The dominance exerted over our lives by this one invention is without
precedent in history. So pervasive is its influence and so inextricably
is it bound up with our way of life and habits of thought that the extent
of its intrusion in our civilization is barely noticed. To insist on seeing
it as no more than one of several alternative schemes of travel, and to
propose a careful assessment of its benefits and costs smacks almost of
the quixotic. Imagine a modern sceptic returning on a Wellsian time-

machine to the second half of the eighteenth century and presenting the following conundrum to Dr Johnson: What gift to mankind is of such worth as to warrant an annual sacrifice of two hundred thousand lives, an annual list of five million people crippled, the transformation of the world's towns and cities into a concrete wasteland made hideous with noise, filth and danger, the dissipation of the countryside, the slow poisoning of the air in town and suburb, the enfeeblement of the health and the corruption of the character of peoples,[1] and the creation of conditions favourable to the generation and execution of crimes of robbery and violence?[2] What reply could the sage give, but that it must be of a nature, sir, that is beyond the bounds of man's imagination.

And what, in fact, may we count as benefits? They are certainly not to be linked with the more salient features that have developed in response to the private automobile: (1) the creation of a *physical* environment in which, while time spent commuting has grown, the motor-car appears increasingly indispensable. For the very existence of a universal private means of transport encourages the geographical dispersion of housing, shopping, entertainment, and consumer services generally. The distinction between suburb and countryside is blurred. Population begins to spread everywhere in a vain bid to 'get away from it all', which further increases the need for the private motor-car. (2) The growth of an *economic* environment that has become closely dependent on the continued popularity of the private motor-car. So large a part of the modern economy is geared to automobile production that it is officially recognized as a barometer for industry as a whole and, indeed, as a fiscal lever in regulating aggregate demand. Worse, the size of the complex of industries involved in producing and maintaining automobiles, to say nothing of the army of car-owners, have given rise to entrenched interests that bar the road to consideration of all radical proposals that appear to threaten their immediate gains.[3] (3) The growth, finally, of a *psy-*

[1] 'As aggression is one of the primary instincts of man, it is not surprising that many drivers under stress become dangerously aggressive, cursing, racing, and "carving up" other drivers. Unfortunately, the motorist's environment is accurately calculated to provoke just this sort of conduct. Anonymity and lack of social contact – the joy of the driver as he speeds along in his sealed tin box – are strongly conducive to aggression.' (Adam Raphael, motoring correspondent of *The Guardian*. *The Guardian*, 17th November, 1967.)

[2] Without the private means of a fast get-away crimes of robbery and violence would have very little chance of success.

[3] According to *The Economist* (11th June, 1966): 'Traffic congestion is Rome's most obvious problem. The old city, with its narrow streets, simply will not take

chological environment, one of almost abject dependence on the automobile; one that has indeed transformed it into a fetish, a sex symbol, a status symbol, and a power symbol.[1]

There is left, then, only the most illusory of all claims, the alleged 'freedom to go where one likes, at any time one likes, and in privacy and comfort'. As though the highways are uncongested! As though driving is a known specific for sweetening the temper and improving the digestion! As though the locust horde of private cars does not destroy, surely and rapidly, the very pleasure, variety and amenity that each is seeking! And when men, knowing all this, can do no more than shrug in resignation one must seriously wonder whether free-will is not, after all, also illusory.

IV

Be that as it may, the clear alternative to the Buchanan Plan emerging from the parable is inescapable. We must begin to think in terms of abandoning all engineering schemes for *accommodating* the mounting road traffic. Instead, we must start evolving schemes for *containing* it. Indeed, the one radical alternative we should take a long look at before contemplating the range of compromise solutions that are feasible is that of a plan for the gradual abolition of all privately owned automobiles.

For a fraction of the money the nation is currently spending on the maintenance of private cars and on the Government services necessary to keep the traffic moving – to say nothing of the cost of all the spillover effects already described – we could simultaneously achieve three desirable objectives: (i) provide a comfortable, frequent and highly

---

the growing flood of private cars. . . . There are brilliant paper plans to stop the chaos but the political courage to carry them out is lacking. A new ring-road is being built, but so far every attempt to discipline traffic in the centre has collapsed at the first contact with vested interests.'

[1] 'The point has not been missed by the car manufacturers. Few car advertisements have ever made so blatant an appeal to masculine aggression as that for the high-powered German Audi saloon – "Power like this tests a man . . . blazing take-off . . . frontal assault" which was withdrawn after a protest from Mrs Castle. Yet much car advertising is still firmly directed towards the gods of virility and violence; for example: "The Hot New Humber Mark II", "The Great '68 Symbol, the Sleek, Scorchy new Victor", and of course the most famous of all, Esso's "Put a Tiger in Your Tank".' (Adam Raphael, *op. cit.*)

efficient public transport service, bus, train, or tube, in all the major population areas (and, in the interest of quiet and clean air, preferably electrically-powered transport),[1] (ii) through government control of public transport, to restrain and gradually reverse the spread of population that has followed in the wake of post-war speculative building and is in the process of transforming the south-east into an uninterrupted suburban region, and (iii) to restore quiet and dignity to our cities, and to enable people to wander unobstructed by traffic and enjoy once more the charm of historic towns and villages.[2]

Further radical changes would, of course, have to be made in the organization of freight delivery if we are successfully to avoid massive investment in refashioning our cities to cater for the growing commercial traffic. The movement of such freight should be minimized: (*a*) by substituting as far as possible existing railways in the built-up areas during off-peak hours; (*b*) similarly, by adapting and extending London's Underground to carry freight, initially during the night; and (*c*) removing freight deliveries from a multitude of small and large firms and placing them instead under a single authority in order, like the post office, to avail ourselves of the economies of co-ordination. Finally, in order to maintain the environment of the city, the possibilities of organizing shop deliveries at times when people are off the streets, say between three and seven in the mornings, deserves careful study.[3]

At any rate – if we are to have a single solution for the country at large –here is one alternative solution towards which we might advance, a radical one to be sure, but technically practicable, and one providing a

[1]The provisional continuation of a taxi service in the metropolis should be conceded (on condition the taxis were fitted with anti-fume devices) in order to prevent abuses arising from any exemption in favour of privileged groups such as doctors or ministers of the crown.

[2]When one considers the reliance on the modern automobile by organized crime, especially by the robbery-and-violence gangs, one is tempted to claim for the scheme an inevitable and immense reduction of city crime.

[3]An outright prohibition against freight deliveries during the day need not be introduced initially in such an experiment. For instance, one could permit vehicles free access during the night hours while imposing a levy on those wishing to use the streets outside these hours. Moreover only electrically-powered vehicles might be allowed with speed limits not exceeding, say, 15 miles per hour.

One incidental advantage to the British consumer of such a scheme would be to encourage shops to hold larger inventories than they do at present. (Shops would, in any case, choose to hold larger inventories if the true costs of currently transporting their goods had to be borne by them.)

relatively inexpensive way, in terms of money and lives,[1] of establishing a more civilized pattern of living.

It is not a solution that will be presented to us by the market, however, and understandably, not one that will be proposed to us by the technocrats, yet it is one that is worthy of consideration by a nation that prides itself on its social awareness and political maturity. In the meantime, local plans to prohibit motor-cars, during certain hours at least, from designated special areas in resorts, historic towns, and city centres – in London, certainly the area about Soho, including Piccadilly Circus and Leicester Square, so that, as in times gone by, people may stroll freely through the city streets enjoying once more the hubbub and gaiety of human voices, and recapturing perhaps a lost sense of community and citizenship – will make some modest contribution towards making the physical environment more enjoyable.

The only alternatives to this radical solution, that are both feasible and inexpensive, are those based on the principle of 'separate facilities', already discussed; in other words the provision of large viable areas for those citizens who want, with varying degrees of intensity, to opt out of the environment of mounting disamenity and disaster created by the private automobile and air travel.

But within the city, at least, there can be no socially acceptable

---

[1]The public should be made aware that in choosing to continue with the present system, in choosing the private car rather than public transport, it also implicitly chooses to sacrifice the lives of many thousands of citizens and to cripple for life a great many more. Currently we write off the lives of over seven thousand men, women and children each year and about ten times that number seriously injured. In the United States, with far greater experience of motoring than we, and with better roads built to carry more traffic at higher speeds, the community has been brought to accept an annual sacrifice of lives now running at fifty-three thousand a year. The sacrifice of a life or two by primitive communities in the belief that it ensured a good harvest seems humane in comparison with the implicit decision to kill some tens of thousands yearly that the pleasures of private motoring be upheld.

The Government, aware of the rising figures, salves its conscience by endlessly exhorting us to be more careful while, at the same time, permitting motor-car manufacturers and oil companies to goad the public, especially the impressionable young, to ever faster speeds. And while the oil companies are urging motorists to 'put tigers in their tanks' the Government connives by imposing unbelievably lenient accident laws. At the time of writing a man who was driving at 60 miles per hour was fined £1,500 for simultaneously killing a woman and her daughter. This works out at £750 per head, a sum that compares favourably with the cost of a licence to kill an elephant in Africa. Yet the newspapers reported that it was the highest fine that had ever been imposed for this offence.

solution to the traffic problem that aims to accommodate the private automobile. Continuation of the present policy of attempting to do so by piecemeal alterations leads ultimately to the crucifixion of the city by its traffic – an epithet that just about describes what has happened in Los Angeles.

Chapter 10

The Transport Economist

Men have become the victims of their faith in progress. Owing to the institutional framework lagging in crucial respects behind economic developments, men are under the illusion that they have freely chosen the private automobile as the conveyance of the future. They have unthinkingly come to accept it as an inescapable fact of modern living. Yet what is really crying out for modernization is not technology but the institutional framework of the economy. Until we succeed in modernizing this institutional framework we shall continue to encounter difficulties in bringing into the terms of choice that people should face a variety of social costs that escape conventional accounting. Under an institutional framework which, among other effects, had that of saddling the motorists with defraying to the full all social costs, including compensatory payments for reducing the amenity of others, the traffic problem would disappear of itself.

One might have hoped that considerations such as these would have been brought to the attention of the public by the so-called transport economist to which, in despair, the Government is now turning for guidance – it being one of the persistent illusions of twentieth-century governments that no social problem can long withstand the combined brain power and know-how of a large enough body of scientists, engineers, statisticians and economists. However it is not just the alleged conflict of purposes in the Ministry of Transport, as between planners, engineers, administrators and economists, that is holding matters up. One may now safely assume that the influence of the transport economist is in the ascendant – a fact which would be heartening if all roads were somehow removed from their environment and situated instead somewhere in the moon or in the more desolate parts of the earth. But since the traffic problem is to be found largely within the cities, towns and suburbs, and the problem is, therefore, one of social welfare in general, the transport economist, as it happens, is not the man to consult. For the transport economist addresses himself in the main to the mutual frustration experienced by the increasing traffic; that is, only to those costs, or diseconomies, that additional traffic impose on existing traffic, and not with costs imposed by traffic as a whole on the rest of society. If he cannot, or will not, measure the latter costs his calculations of the rates of return on existing roads, of the benefit-cost ratios of traffic investment, and of the 'optimal traffic flows' within towns and cities, remain without allocative significance.

To be plain, the expertise that the transport economist can bring to bear on traffic problems in town and city is largely bogus. I do not allege that he is consciously perpetrating a fraud. Like all too many men in the social sciences he is impatient to display his scientific credentials, anxious to be seen measuring, that is, even where it entails, as it so manifestly does in this case, measuring much the smaller part of the problem for lack of a method to capture the larger. Since I wish these allegations to be taken seriously I shall spell them out carefully to avoid any misunderstanding.

First, then, it is alleged that the transport economist by and large confines his models to measuring the costs on traffic generated by traffic (mutual congestion costs) and ignores or relegates to parenthetical remarks the widespread accumulation of effects on the environment; not only the dirt and dust, the noise and smell, and the distraction and tenseness caused by the uninterrupted pressure of traffic always about us, but also the growing dehumanization of the physical environment in response to mounting traffic. Roads and buildings are constructed with the needs of motorized traffic in mind, not of pedestrians. He ignores also the role of the motor-car as the chief instrument, in the post-war period, for spreading subtopia over the countryside of Britain. These social costs, it may be alleged, arise from repercussions that are so widespread and interconnected as to defy, at present, any acceptable method of valuation. But to ignore them in all decisions bearing on road traffic is irresponsible. At a guess, I should put the measurable congestion costs of the transport economist at not more than one-twentieth of the total of social costs generated by motorized traffic, the remaining nineteen-twentieths being accounted for by the so-called intangibles. Whether or not others go along with these impressionistic figures, no one, surely, will deny the evidence of his senses which tells him that the private automobile is the most potent influence since the war in shaping the environment around us.

Second, the device employed for measuring benefits to the motoring population is perverse. No matter what their degree of sophistication very few of the commonly used transport models fail to draw on the notion of 'consumers' surplus' – a measure that is approximately represented by the area under the price-demand curve – as an indicator of benefits. Whether they are concerned with: (a) benefit-cost ratios; (b) the internal rate of return on a new road or bridge; or, (c) the determination of the so-called 'optimal traffic flow' (a procedure that takes account of the congestion costs imposed by each additional vehicle on the traffic as a whole), this measure of consumers' surplus is, generally, an essential part of the calculation.

Yet the 'consumers' surplus' measure of benefit can be used as an approximation only under peculiarly restrictive conditions, particular attention being paid to the constancy of the alternative opportunities available. By neglecting this crucial condition the resulting measure of consumers' surplus is not merely unreliable. In the circumstances in which it is used by transport economists it is possible, even likely, that the resulting measure of benefit is *inversely* related to the actual benefit: thus, as the welfare of the motoring population declines the consumers' surplus measure may well register increasing benefit – a contingency that may have escaped the attention of transport economists. For this reason I have discussed it more formally in Appendix C.

II

Before moving on, let us illustrate the nature of two interrelated kinds of decision necessary to uncover a range of separate-facilities opportunities that are alternative to the over-all solution proposed in the preceding part of this digression.

(A) First, there are decisions to be taken about the particular features of traffic control within any area, which may involve one or more of the following: at one extreme (i) all motorized transport of any description to be excluded; (ii) only public transport permitted supplemented, or not, by a taxi service; (iii) commercial vehicles within the precincts of the city, town, or suburb, not permitted during the day; (iv) commercial vehicles permitted if electrically powered, with or without extra charge; (v) whatever traffic permitted, all of it subject to drastic speed limits; (vi) permitted traffic confined to certain roads; (vii) Post Office to take over and co-ordinate all freight deliveries.

(B) Second, there have to be decisions about the size of the areas themselves over which any of the above features, or combination of such features, is to be established. (i) The minimum non-motoring area could, of course, be no smaller than a conventional pedestrian precinct found within certain towns or suburbs; (ii) in addition, ancient, winding, or narrow streets, or secluded squares could be set aside purely for the convenience of pedestrians; (iii) central parts of some cities and towns, and the more picturesque and historic parts, could be cleared of all motorized traffic; (iv) some town and city centres entire could be freed of all private and commercial traffic; (v) some cities, towns and suburbs may be freed wholly of all private motoring; (vi) select regions, districts, and whole counties might be made available for all those wishing to escape the proximity and consequences of private motoring and air travel.

A number of difficult decisions must inevitably crop up in arranging the transition from the present unrelieved traffic nightmare to any one of a variety of solutions. Since I am pointing out the main features of a solution and not presenting a blueprint to the Government I shall not discuss them here – though it need never be doubted that those who feel their interests threatened will make the most of them to prevent a change of direction from the present policy of drift into traffic chaos. However, the precondition of any social advance is that people become convinced of the existence of many practical alternatives to the present policy, alternatives offering a wide range of choice hitherto denied them in that most vital of influences affecting their welfare, the physical environment itself in which they dwell and work.

Chapter 11

Social Conflict

I

Clearly, unresolved adverse spillover effects imply an opposition of interest between the generator of such effects and the recipients. But where the opposing groups involved are large and easily identified the conflict of interest may assume a broader social dimension, a feature illustrated by certain conspicuous spillover effects associated closely with post-war affluence. One that is coming to a head just now in the United States is the conflict between those commercial enterprises that for years have been pouring their waste products into the once-fresh waters of lakes and rivers, on the one hand, and the public at large on the other – a fact of life that is being belatedly discovered by journalists and by citizens who are being deprived of the use of such waters for drinking, fishing or bathing. A couple of years ago the city of New York, at that time apprehensive of an impending water shortage, discovered that it could no longer tap the obvious source of supply, the Hudson River, which is now poisonous from years of cumulative effluents. Of course, if it were otherwise, if fresh water were everywhere abundant – which has been the prevailing conviction in this country and in the United States until very recently – there might be no good reason why it should not be used wastefully and fouled by industry. In view of the extent and growth of water pollution, however, it may be simpler to enact general laws against fouling fresh water, spoiling beaches with oil, sewage, and so on, rather than to attempt to regulate waste-disposal of this sort either by the amenity-rights formulation or by complicated formulae intended to realize an ideal correction. The West is sufficiently rich to make amends for past follies by erring, if at all, on the generous

side in the task of preserving for posterity those limited natural resources which, in the absence of prohibiting legislation or controls,
would continue to be spoiled and squandered.

II

A more menacing source of conflict at this stage in world history,
though people appear reluctant to recognize the fact, is that arising from
continued population expansion and, more recently, mass migration. In
very poor countries, such as India, the 'classical' economic situation is
still to be found: a growing population pressing on limited natural
resources, and a tendency, therefore, for the incomes of property-
owners to rise while, in general, living standards settle near bare subsistence. Although this Malthusian situation is a thing of the past within
Western Europe, there still remains the potent threat of further movements of indigenous population, in particular of motorized population,
into urban areas. Such movements continue to press on limited space as
to make the physical environment in which we live increasingly
disagreeable.

To financial columnists and growthmen, on the other hand, one of
the factors insistently stressed as being conducive to rapid economic expansion is an increase of population, whether the increase is a result
mainly of indigenous population growth or of immigration. On this view,
it is not so much *per capita* 'real' growth that is desirable but *total*
economic growth of the country. A growth-obsessed government setting
itself the task of increasing aggregate national product by, say, 25 per
cent over some short period can be tempted to achieve its goal more
simply by importing labour, even if imported labour happens to be less
efficient and less adaptable than indigenous labour. Those who have
gone overboard in their passion for growth, as have influential persons
in the Common Market countries, do not hesitate at the idea of augmenting population from outside countries. And certainly one need
anticipate no opposition from the business world, whose interests are
served by an expanding market however brought about, nor from land-
lords who contemplate with equanimity the rise in rents caused by the
competition of an increasing population for a fixed supply of land.[1]

[1] Rising economic rents and rising site values in response to population pressure is one way of coping with the spillover effects resulting from an increasing
number of people seeking to settle within a given area. Though a well-functioning

True, freedom to move, to migrate to other lands, is an ancient and cherished freedom. Its value stems from a presumed diversity of conditions as between different countries. The appearance of some degree of civil and political liberty in other countries acts to set limits to the civil and political oppression a man will endure in his native land. The existence of other countries in which land is abudant and fertile, and in which economic prospects are more hopeful, provides opportunities of a materially better life for those who, through no fault of their own, were born into the poorer regions of the globe.

Significant political differences between countries there still are. But the numbers seeking to migrate for political reasons are, at present, trivially small compared with those who would migrate for economic reasons. And here the sad but inescapable fact is that what holds true for one period of history will not necessarily hold true for another. And what, at any moment of time, holds true for the movement of a few thousand families does not hold true for a movement of a few million. There comes a point in the scale of immigration after which it has a perceptible impact on the character of the host country: not only on its economy, but on its political life, on its society and general amenity – all matters of legitimate concern to the indigenous population. The most ardent internationalist cannot fail to recognize that the extension of economic opportunity to the potential migrant, a good thing in itself, may conflict with the economic opportunities of the indigenous population; that the improved welfare of the former may be bought only at the expense of the latter; and that, especially in localities favoured by immigrants, the initial exhilaration and high hopes of the one group may be the occasion of sorrow and resentment of the other.[1]

---

market acts to promote 'optimal' adjustment in respect of this particular spillover, the higher cost of living suffered by non-landowners may be a source of conflict.

The reader should be clear that the achievement of 'optimality' is no assurance against a worsening situation. 'Optimality' makes the 'best' of any situation, whether it is improving or worsening. If, because of immigrant inflow, the amount of land per inhabitant declines there will exist, notwithstanding an optimal 'exploitation' of land, a divergence of material interests between the existing number of inhabitants and the potential immigrants. The material interests for wealthy but small countries may, however, be less important than its interest in preserving amenity and social harmony.

[1] It should be evident by now that Anglo-Saxon countries do not lend themselves easily to the process of racial integration – at least not on a large scale. While there can be differences of opinion on the causes of, and remedies for,

In particular, mass migration from the poorer countries of Asia and Africa into the countries of Western Europe appears to be fraught with social and economic consequences not all of which are congenial to their indigenous populations. There are no longer vast inhabitable areas to be peopled in Western Europe. Inasmuch as a net inflow of migrants acts to reduce the amount of land *per capita* available, real rents must rise; inasmuch as immigrants from poor countries are for the most part unskilled and without capital assets there is an initial reduction in the capital-income ratio of the host country. Furthermore, since net immigration raises rents and profits relative to wages, it is a force tending to increase the inequality of incomes.[1]

Finally, large-scale immigration is not only likely to be socially unsettling, in an economy as close to full employment as the United Kingdom has been since the war, it is almost sure to have a net inflationary impact on the economy.[2] A large-scale inflow of relatively unskilled labour therefore acts as a distributionally regressive force (inasmuch as profits and, to a lesser extent, wages increase at the expense of fixed income groups including pensioners). In addition, an increase of population from abroad, like an increase in the indigenous population, raises the demand for imports (even in the complete absence of upward pressure

---

colour prejudice it must be conceded, again, that the pre-condition for active antagonism is the existence of an immigrant population of some minimal size – a minimal size which depends upon the identifiability of the immigrant groups and their degree of dispersion throughout the country. For the coloured immigrants into Britain, this minimal size has apparently been exceeded some years ago. Today an unprejudiced observer could hardly deny that the help Britain affords through absorbing immigrants from the economically underprivileged multitudes of Asia and Africa is slight. Nor could he deny that the potential for social disturbance and disamenity in this country is significant. In these circumstances, it needs more than ordinary philosophy to hope for a balance of gain in the foreseeable future. The tendency for a once relatively homogeneous and politically mature society to become increasingly immersed in the anxieties of racial conflict will sadden many good liberals. One of the less recognized consequences is that it diverts the country's attention from those urgent problems connected with economic growth which form the main theme of this book.

The transformation of a well-integrated nation state into a multi-racial society does not appear to be a necessary phase in its historical development nor, at the present time, a clearly desirable social objective.

[1] The extent of this tendency depends on the scale of immigration, its quality and adaptability, also on the rate of capital accumulation, the innovating process, and the technical difficulty of substituting labour for capital in industry.

[2] For some estimates of excess primary aggregate demand generated by immigration, see 'Immigration: Some Economic Effects' by Mishan and Needleman in *Lloyds Bank Review*, July 1966.

on domestic prices) without inducing a corresponding increase of exports thereby worsening the balance-of-payments position – or worsening the terms of trade in the longer run.[1] None the less, I am inclined to rate very much higher than these untoward economic effects the impact of large-scale immigration on the existing spillover effects of an already too-large-for-comfort population and the already intractable traffic problem. These spillovers will necessarily be aggravated, and frequently localized, by immigration into this rather tight little island.[2]

It may be observed in passing that this conflict between the existing inhabitants of a region and would-be immigrants is also to be found within the frontiers of a single country. For instance, according to Professor Raymond Dasmann,[3] the beauty and natural resources of California are being destroyed by the rapid influx of Americans from other States. 'Everywhere', writes Dasmann, 'crowding destroys the values that the people who crowd in come to seek.' Lake Tahoe, the largest and perhaps the most beautiful mountain lake in the United States, became the fashionable place to go to after the Second World War. 'Nevada gamblers began to build skyscraper hotels. . . . Seepage and effluent from sewage treatment plants began to pour . . . into the once clear water.' Now, like other lakes in the United States, Tahoe is on its way to becoming an algae-fouled cesspool.

[1] It is sometimes argued in the popular press that this country benefits from immigrants' willingness to enter unpopular occupations where services are maintained without raising costs to the public. This is however, a one-sided analysis. When account is taken of the domestic opportunities for improved allocation in the absence of immigration the argument no longer holds. This topic among others has been discussed by Dr Needleman and myself in _Lloyds Bank Review_, January 1968.

[2] It is a sad reflection on our times that scientists interested in the 'population explosion' are concerned for the most part with the purely technical problem of feeding the swelling populations. Schemes range from more high-powered animal farms to processing grass, and from exploiting the seas to making plastic meat substitutes.

That already man has broken all ecological bounds and that, unless one can somehow reverse the trends, the world's population will have doubled by the end of the century; that thereafter we shall be as thick as locusts over many parts of the inhabitable earth – all this is as nothing to the vision of growthmen who continue to exorcize any future spectre with the word challenge.

[3] Raymond F. Dasmann, _The Destruction of California_ (Macmillan, 1965). In an endeavour to check the gradually declining quality of life in California, Dasmann suggests a stop to the building of more freeways, power stations, and residential accommodation in order to discourage potential immigrants. Needless to relate, California's businessmen and government officials have brushed aside any solution inimical to those profiting from the business boom.

III

From the destruction wrought by large population movements to that wrought by mass tourism is a short step and one that opens up a vista of the immeasurable destructive potential of indiscriminate economic growth. In the last decade alone there has been something of a holocaust of the scarcest of our earthly resources, natural beauty. In this instance the conflict of interest is between, on the one hand, the tourists, tourist agencies, traffic industries and ancillary services, to say nothing of governments anxious to augment their reserves of foreign currencies, and all those who care about preserving natural beauty on the other.

There is obviously also a conflict of interest between present and future generations. It is true that a sizeable fraction of mankind form part of regular tourist invasion, but this is the result of pricing travel well below the social costs incurred. For the cost to the marginal tourist takes no account of the additional congestion costs he imposes or all others (tourists and inhabitants), or of the additional loss of quiet and fresh air, or of the scenic destruction suffered by all in consequence of additional building required. Moreover, it is clear to the most revent nature-lover, that any personal sacrifice he makes will have no practical effect in reducing mass tourism, any more than his refusal to drive an automobile would reverse the trend towards increasing city congestion. If anything, there is an incentive for him to travel the sooner, and the more frequently, before the potential tourist haunt in question is irredeemably ruined – to 'enjoy it before the crowds get there', as the advertisement bids us. As things are then the tourist trade, in a competitive scramble to uncover all places of once quiet repose, of wonder, beauty and historic interest to the money-flushed multitude, is in effect literally and irrevocably destroying them. Once serene and lovely towns such as Andorra[1] and Biarritz are smothered with new hotels and the

[1] Several years ago, a correspondent in the Pyrenees wrote for *The Economist* (22nd August, 1959) a short piece on 'The Last Days of Andorra'. He observed that tourists still went to Andorra in search of the exotic . . . 'to see its mediaeval houses and bridges, fine Romanesque church towers and unsullied mountain vistas; to enjoy its eyrie-like calm and pure air. As a result of the tourist invasion, however, Andorra's air is at the moment a nicely balanced blend of exhaust fumes and cement dust, vibrant with the competing *chachachas* of Radio-Andorra and Andorradio; parking is the same kind of problem as in London; and every other beauty-spot is pock-marked with hotels, bungalows and camping sites. One of the loveliest church towers in the country, that at Ordino, has been dwarfed by a graceless new block sited exactly six inches from it.

dust and roar of motorized traffic. The isles of Greece have become a sprinkling of lidos in the Aegean Sea. Delphi is ringed with shiny new hotels. In Italy the real estate man is responsible for atrocities exemplified by the skyscraper approach to Rome seen across the Campagna, while the annual invasion of tourists has transformed once-famous resorts, Rapallo, Capri, Alassio and scores of others, before the last war no less enchanting, into so many vulgar Coney Islands.

None the less the tourist agency continues to conjure up for the young and gullible visions of far-away places, mysterious, romantic, primitive even, to be enjoyed with all 'mod cons' at a cheap package price. Others regard the swelling avalanche of tourists as a great democratic achievement, a unifying force in the world, a growing opportunity for all people 'to see the world and to perceive its life and art'. But, like extending the opportunity to motor into the centre of London to every car-owner in the country, it is a purely illusory opportunity. Travel on this scale, with the annual need to accommodate millions of young people, all anxious to cram their fortnight with approved experiences, rapidly and inevitably disrupts the character of the affected regions, the character of their populations, and their ways of living. As swarms of holiday-makers arrive by air, sea and land, by coach, train and private car, hot in pursuit of recreation; as concrete is poured over the earth; as hotels, caravans, casinos, night-clubs, chalets and blocks of sun-flats crowd into the area and retreat into the hinterland, local life and industry shrivel, hospitality vanishes, and indigenous populations drift into a quasi-parasitic way of life catering with contemptuous servility to the unsophisticated multitude.

The issue is not at all that of aristocratic privilege versus democratic freedom, not even that of the genuine connoisseur versus the philistine hordes. Geographical space, the choicest bits of it anyway, form one of the strictly limited resources of this now tiny planet. And – as in so many other things – what a few may enjoy in freedom the crowd necessarily destroys for itself. Notwithstanding which, under present institutional arrangements (since there is certainly a lot more money to be earned in

---

'. . . Building sites are being snapped up in Andorra-la-Vella at £25 a square yard. At the present rate of development the whole central valley from Encamp to Santa Julia will soon be one unbroken ribbon of flamboyant façades.'

With slight alterations, this passage would summarize the recent history of hundreds of favourite resorts in France, Italy, Spain, Greece and other Mediterranean countries.

promoting this process of rapid erosion) unless international agreement can be reached to control further tourist damage our children will inherit a world almost wholly bereft of places of undisturbed natural beauty.[1]

One policy measure alone which would go far to reverse this dismal trend may be hazarded: an international ban against all air travel. With more leisurely travel habits restored – and enforced by prohibiting speeds in excess, say, of 30 knots – one could confidentially anticipate an enormous reduction in the demand for foreign travel. With equal confidence one could predict an outcry by the interested parties against the adoption of so drastic ('impracticable', 'irresponsible', 'reactionary') a proposal.

But what is the alternative? To continue to drift along? We have already, and within a few short post-war years, all but destroyed a heritage of tranquil unmarred natural beauty that had else endured the passage of centuries and millennia. With a hubris unmatched since the heyday of Victorian capitalism and with a blindness peculiar to our own time, we have abandoned ourselves to ransacking the most precious and irreplaceable good the earth provides, without thought to the desolation of the future and to the deprivation of posterity.

A more diluted version of this proposal, one drawing its rationale from the separate-facilities solution, would be to remove all possibility of swift travel service – which usually means air travel – to a wide selection of mountain lake and coastal resorts and islands scattered about the globe; and within and around them to abolish all motorized traffic. Areas should be side aside for the true lover of natural beauty who is prepared to make his pilgrimage by boat and willing to explore islands, valleys, bays, and woodlands on foot or by horse-drawn vehicles.

---

[1] Robert Graves in an extract from his book *Majorca Observed* printed in *The Telegraph* colour supplement (14th May, 1965) begins as follows: 'Only fifteen years ago a *New Yorker* cartoon showed an old lady asking her travel agent: "Whatever happened to those nice cheap little islands in the Mediterranean that you used to advertise before the war?" Yet nobody foresaw the brand-new phenomenon of mass-tourism – meaning charter-flights, block-booking of hotels, and so clever a rationalizing of ways and means that a fortnight's holiday would cost no more than an individual return air-fare. This business now brings 5,000 planes a month to a new and vastly enlarged Palma airport every summer, and has encouraged the building of over 1,000 new hotels.'

Part IV

National Income and National Welfare: A False Equation

Chapter 12

The Myth of Consumers' Sovereignty

I

So far the critique of economic growth as a social priority has been developed within a framework of basic assumptions familiar to economists. Within such a framework it would be possible to interpret the operation of a highly competitive economy as one tending to bring scarce resources into relation with people's wants – but only in the absence of unresolved spillover effects. Once we qualify these basic assumptions to accord more closely with the facts of everyday experience, the rationale of the economic system and, therefore, the social justification of economic growth, begin to look very shaky.

One basic assumption frequently invoked to vindicate economic growth is that any extension of the *effective* range of choice facing a person (whether presented to him through the market or directly by the Government) adds to his welfare. The word effective here indicates that any additional economic opportunities facing him – such as a rise in the price of the services he sells, or a fall in the prices of the goods that he buys – will induce him to select a new combination of services and goods notwithstanding that the old combination is still available to him.[1] In the

[1]This assumption, equating enlargement of effective choice with improved welfare, is closely connected with the assumption that the consumer knows his own interest best. This latter assumption is one which favours 'free choice' as against 'paternalism' in the distribution of goods. In so far as government taxation (in order to provide goods or services) can be interpreted as a spending of people's money for them on goods or services that could be produced and/or distributed as economically through the market, one may legitimately talk of 'paternalism'. If the liberal economist ascribes a higher utility to a batch of goods that is freely chosen than to one of the same value that is, to some extent, prescribed by the Government he does so on the grounds that a man knows

following chapter it will be argued that this assumption is far from plausible. In the meantime we may suggest that technological innovation need not result, in the first place, in any effective extension of choice.

Now a person can choose only from those goods and services that are offered to him on the market. And a range of alternative physical environments (mentioned in the preceding chapters) is not the only thing the market fails to provide. Though perhaps of less importance, the appearance of new goods or new models of existing goods on the market is all too often the occasion of a withdrawal of the older goods or models. The customer will search for them in vain. They are withdrawn from production at the discretion of the producer.

More important yet are the restrictions placed on a man's choice of occupation by existing technology and institutions. The older liberal economist would argue that just as the individual chooses, as consumer, to buy various amounts of the goods offered by the market, so also, as the owner of productive services, he is guided by market prices in offering various amounts of his services in different occupations. This symmetry is obviously forced on the analysis in the interests of elegance and mathematical convenience. It may be that in some imaginary economy a person could spread his work among a variety of occupations on the familiar equi-marginal principle in the same way as he is deemed to spread his income among the goods offered to him by the market. But modern industry is not so accommodating, and for the superficially good reason that if a man were allowed to choose in this way – choosing each day to put a few hours in this occupation and a few hours in that – the productivity of the economy could not be maintained. The employee has therefore to choose his work subject, for the most part, to the condition that he conform exactly to the working week of the firm.

In the narrow growth sense, one in which social welfare is measured directly by output, such a constraint on working hours may appear

---

his own interests better than anyone else. The question of the empirical truth of this proposition may be held to be secondary to the political belief that we should act *as if* people did know their own interests best since actions based on other premises would be liable to result in undesirable social and political consequences. It is also possible, however, to regard the proposition as a *factual* assumption about human behaviour – a hypothesis that free choice always, or usually, or sooner or later, brings about a greater access of welfare to the individual than would be obtained under any system that restricted his freedom of choice.

necessary. But if the economist is interested in social welfare rather than in physical output he must concern himself with the burden of this constraint on the worker's choice in a modern economy that is almost wholly consumer oriented – and, indeed, the private enterprise system is generally vindicated by reference to the individual's satisfaction *qua* consumer while neglecting his satisfaction *qua* worker. It is, of course, easy to forget that the individual may have occupational wants independent of technical progress since, over time, he is seen to adapt himself to whatever technological means are available. Though we suppose him, at any moment of time, to have a set of preferences among existing occupational opportunities, there is no use in comparing his preferences between newly adopted and obsolete methods inasmuch as he is rapidly deprived of any choice of the latter. The economist has no means of discovering what changes in welfare, if any, result from a change-over from one technology to another.

Yet something may be said. The tedium of repetitive work in modern industry, even that of watching a screen and turning knobs, is easy to underestimate by those fortunate to escape such tasks. One has only to reflect on the efforts and the expenditure incurred by large numbers of people in combating the monotony of their daily occupation, their growing eagerness to engage in all manner of hobbies in their spare time, their desire to recapture a feeling of craftsmanship or creativity – one has only to reflect on these things to discern opportunities for social gain in making existing industrial arrangements more flexible. Nor need one contemplate a clear choice between the existing highly organized system of production and the extreme alternative of uninhibited choice in respect of hours of work and variety. One need only admit the clear possibility of social gain, after full allowance has been made for the consequent reduction in physical output, of extending to people of all ages a much wider choice in the hours of work, a wider geographical choice in the location of smaller units of industry and, above all, a wider choice in the methods of production. Experiment on such lines is obviously inconsistent with any criterion of technical efficiency: some material remuneration would have to be sacrificed in the conscious pursuit of ways and means of deriving positive enjoyment, stimulation, and companionship in one's daily occupation. Indeed, this proposal may be recognized as an instance of the separate facilities concept for promoting welfare. Not everyone would wish to sacrifice efficiency, and therefore earnings, in exchange for more of these other desirable factors. But there should be enough people capable of enriching their lives by such arrangements to justify the experiment.

Measured by the conventional index of finished goods, the implementation of such proposals may well involve negative economic growth. That an increase in social welfare – an increase in the range of effective choice – may be brought about by negative economic growth may appear paradoxical, if not infuriating, to some growthmen. But that is because they are interested in social welfare only in so far as it seems to justify economic growth, and not the other way about, as they sometimes pretend.

II

A second basic assumption of the economist engaged in measuring changes in welfare, or 'the standard of living', is that the institutional constraints under which choices are made do not alter over time. In so far as they do change over time there can be changes in welfare also, for better or for worse.

Over the decision most vital of all to his well-being, the epoch and society wherein he lives, the individual alas is unable to exercise any choice whatsoever. Born into a certain social and physical *milieu*, born into a certain home, much of the pattern of his life follows as a matter of course. Many of the consequences that arise from nature and nurture, from inherited natural endowments and from upbringing, he will be powerless to influence. Within limits determined by these consequences he is, later, free to choose an occupation but, having adopted it, the material choices that he exercises through the market are thereafter somewhat narrowly conscribed. If, for example, be becomes a stockbroker or bank manager in the City, his choice of clothes, car, residence, even his choice of food and entertainment, will not differ markedly from that of his colleagues. The conventions followed by friends, associates, and customers will continually weigh with him unless he is ready to forfeit their good opinion of his character and soundness upon which his success depends.

Such trite observations take on significance as the cost of keeping in fashion increases with economic growth. Women's fashions are only a more familiar case in point. Popular articles assert that women positively enjoy being in the fashion – though their pleasure, one imagines, may sometimes be traced to a dread of being seen out of fashion. But for most women it would surely be less costly and less exacting to be subject to fashions that changed less frequently. The choice of the pace of fashion, surely a crucial choice, is not open to the individual, only to society as a whole where, at present, it is left entirely to commercial interests to exploit to the limit of technical feasibility. The fashion industry is the prime example of an activity dedicated to using up resources, not to create satisfactions, but to create dissatisfactions with what people possess – in effect to create obsolescence in otherwise perfectly satis-factory goods. Though it has been doing this for ages, it is the increasing frequency of fashion change, and its extension to many articles other than clothes, that is disturbing. Following the lead of United States manufacturers, we are extending the pace of fashion to automobiles, furniture, hardware and electrical goods. Any practical proposals to regulate the rate of change of fashion in clothes and in durable goods may attract a great deal of public support. The would-be pace-setters would, of course, be deprived of approved opportunities for self-display, but the potential saving in national resources should more than suffice to compensate them.

Turning to the range of goods in the economy, though producers use up resources in creating markets for their goods, they are not permitted to produce any goods they wish for which a market might be created. Existing institutions place limits also on the kinds of goods that will be demanded. A wide variety of drugs, weapons, pornographic literature and entertainment, at present illegal and therefore costly, would be readily available at competitive prices in the absence of existing pro-hibitions. Men and women might agree to sell themselves or their children into slavery for certain tangible benefits if the law permitted the institution. In a country having a conscript army, the Government would have no difficulty in promoting a flourishing market in draft tickets, the richer young men effectively buying their way out of national service to the ostensible benefit of both buyer and seller. Again, if speed limits on our roads were limited to a maximum of 15 miles per hour people's choices would change radically not only in respect of auto-mobiles used, and mode of travel, but also in their choice of residence, in their use of time, and in our design of towns and cities and roads. If the penalty for accidentally killing pedestrians were not merely a fine, as at present, but hanging by the neck, one could predict with confidence, a vast change-over to public transport, a voluntary though drastic diminution of speeds, and a quite magical reduction of deaths through

Technology and Growth

traffic accidents. Too much attention has been paid to the concept of expanding choice and too little to the power of legislation in altering, for better or worse, the kind of choices that people make.

III

A third basic assumption required in order to estimate changes in welfare, that the tastes of consumers can be accepted as remaining the same over time, is the least reasonable. But it is fundamental to any such estimates. If a man's given wants are met over time by more or better goods, a *prima facie* case can be made for his being better off. If, on the other hand, his wants change – either because he becomes greedier or because he now seeks a quite different assortment of goods without there being any change in prices – the basis necessary for comparing his satisfaction over time dissolves. And the more rapidly tastes change the less valid is it to infer that rising *per capita* output issues in rising *per capita* welfare.

It is evident, however, that in advanced economies tastes do change rapidly – if only because consumers' wants do not exist independently of the products created by industrial concerns. Indeed, this is just what makes it so misleading to talk of the market as acting to adapt the given resources of the economy to meet the material requirements of society. In fact, not only do producers determine the range of market goods from which consumers must take their choice, they also seek continuously to persuade consumers[1] to choose that which is being produced today and to 'unchoose' that which was being produced yesterday. Therefore to

[1] Admittedly it is difficult in many circumstances to separate the informative from the persuasive elements of an advertisement, to say nothing of gauging the accuracy or relevance of the information provided. 'Smart people smoke Cancerettes!' is a claim which is not easy to test. If we defined the class of smart people we may discover that, in consequence of a prolonged and intensive advertising campaign, smart people have indeed taken to smoking Cancerette cigarettes even though they could not be distinguished from other brands when labels were removed. A picture of the product, or the name of the brand, printed without comment may well persuade people to buy more of the product. However, a case for the abolition of commercial advertising does not depend on such a distinction. Moreover, the abolition of commercial advertising cannot seriously be construed as an infringement of libertarian principle.

All that which is relevant in enabling the public to make a rational choice from the range of material goods and services offered by private enterprise may be more economically conveyed by an impartial body of analysts and administrators – an official or semi-official Consumers' Union in fact. One great

continue to regard the market in an affluent and growing economy as primarily a 'want-satisfying' mechanism is to close one's eyes to the more important fact that it has also become a want-*creating* mechanism.

This fact would be too obvious to mention except that its implications are seldom faced. Over time, an unchanging pattern of wants would just not suffice to absorb the rapid growth in the flow of consumer goods coming on to the domestic markets of rich countries, the United States market in particular. The sustained rise in consumption expenditure at all levels of society depends largely on the unflagging zeal and enterprise of the advertising industry.[1] In its absence, leisure would certainly be increasing faster than it is.

The nation's resources then continue to be used in part to create new wants. These new wants may be deemed imaginary or they may be alleged to be as 'real' as the original set of wants. What cannot be gainsaid, however, is that the foundation necessary to enable economists to infer and measure increases in individual or social welfare crumbles up in these circumstances. Only as given wants remain constant and productive activity serves to narrow the margin of discontent between appetites and their gratifications are we justified in talking of an increase of welfare. And one may reasonably conjecture that unremitting efforts

---

argument in favour of this solution is the large saving in resources, both those expended by commerce (much of it in 'counter-advertising') and those wasted by the public as a result of unsatisfactory choices.

[1] The view that commercial advertising lowers the price of newspapers and journals deserves a comment. In the last resort the full economic costs of newspapers have to be borne by the public at large. But whether they end up paying for a large part of the newspaper through their purchases of the goods that are advertised, as at present, or whether, as an alternative possibility, they pay the full cost of the newspaper, free of commercial advertising while at the same time paying less for goods no longer advertised, is mainly a question of distribution. If we ignore the costs of real resources used in advertising – the services performed by advertising agencies, additional newsprint, etc. – it is purely a question of distribution; those people who buy more of the advertised products effectively subsidizing those newspaper readers who buy less of them. Once the real resources used up in advertising are brought into account, however, the public is paying more for both advertised goods and newspapers combined than it would pay for them in the absence of advertising.

The contribution of advertising, in terms of 'information' and 'entertainment' currently provided to the public, is not large relative to the resources used. Certaintly the flow of relevant and impartial information could be multiplied and made available to the public for a fraction of the resources currently employed in the advertising industry.

directed towards stimulating aspirations and enlarging appetites may cause them to grow faster than the possibilities for their gratification, so increasing over time the margin of social discontent.

Be that as it may, in high consumption economies such as the United States, the trend is for more goods, including hardware, to become fashion goods. Manufacturers strive to create an atmosphere which simultaneously glorifies the 'pace-setter' and derides the fashion laggards. As productivity increases without a commensurate increase in leisure the accent shifts ever more stridently to boost consumption – not least to boost automobile sales although cities and suburbs are near-strangled with traffic – in order, apparently, to maintain output and employment. The economic order is accommodating itself to an indigestible flow of consumer gadgetry by inverting the rationale of its existence: 'scarce wants' have somehow to be created and brought into relation with rising industrial capacity.

Under such perverse conditions growthmen may continue to so juggle with words as to equate economic growth with 'enrichment', or 'civilization', or any other thrice-blessed word. But it is just not possible for the economist to establish a positive link between economic growth and human welfare.

Chapter 13

Weak Links Between Effective
Choice and Welfare

I

In the preceding chapter we accepted, provisionally, the existence of a positive relation between effective choice and welfare, and restricted ourselves to revealing some of the limitations on effective choice under present institutions. The time has come to disabuse the reader of any further belief in this relationship.

First of all, although we have already drawn attention to the impracticability of measuring changes of welfare over time in an economy devoting resources, successfully, to altering people's tastes, even if we supposed, instead, that somehow tastes did remain unaltered, such a relationship between effective choice and welfare is by no means self-evident – at least not in the affluent society. In such a society, one of the chief manifestations of affluence is the steady increase in the number of brands and models of already popular goods. The task of choosing in a rational way, on each occasion, one brand or model from a bewildering and ever-changing array of goods – that is, to weigh up the relative merits of quality, taste, appearance, performance, longevity and other characteristics with respect to a range of prices for each of some several score objects all purporting to serve the same need – would be too time-consuming and too exhausting an occupation even if the entire staff of a consumers' advisory board were placed at the customer's disposal. In the event, there are many things a person buys from habit and much else that is bought on impulse. For all choices that involve fairly large outlays on durable goods, however, the process of choosing is itself a time-consuming business, one that is not made easier by the trend towards more rapid obsolescence of existing models.

It may seem, on superficial reflection, that no person need inconvenience himself if he does not want to; he can always reach out and take the first thing that catches his eye or he can adhere to his customary brand – if it remains available. One can call this a rational solution if he wishes, but it is one that affords little consolation. As the pace of fashion accelerates, as goods become technically more complex and their variety proliferates, the plain fact is that ordinary people do become apprehensive about the increasing possibilities of choosing the wrong thing.[1] If, therefore, an independent panel were given the task of radically reducing the existing prolific variety of goods on the market to a few clearly differentiated types of each good, one could reasonably anticipate a saving of time and some elimination of anxiety, to say nothing of a potential decline of manufacturing costs arising from the resulting standardization of products.

II

If the link between effective choice and welfare does not already appear tenuous, we can go further. The political philosophy of John Stuart Mill may suggest to some that if a man has a mind to drink himself to death no intervention other than that of persuasion is called for. It is thought better (in some political sense) that a man act unwisely of his own free will – provided, always, his action harms no other persons – than that

[1] If, beginning with a situation in which only one kind of shirt were available, a man was transposed to another in which ten different kinds were offered to him, including the old kind, he could of course continue to buy the old kind of shirt. But it does not follow that, if he elects to do this, he is no worse off in the new situation. In the first place, he is aware that he is now *rejecting* nine different kinds of shirts whose qualities he has not compared. The decision to ignore the other nine shirts is itself a cost, and inasmuch as additional shirts continue to come on to the market, and some are withdrawn, he is being subjected to a continual process of decision-taking even though he is able, and willing, to buy the same shirt. In the second place, unless he is impervious to fashion, he will feel increasingly uncomfortable in the old shirt. It is more likely that he will be tempted, then, to risk spending an unpredictable amount of time and trouble in the hope of finding a more suitable shirt.

Moreover, in continuing to review his choice in the light of additional variety and additional information, he is not gradually approaching the choice of some ideal shirt. Since fashions are changing, and since his tastes are being influenced by advertisements, the expenditure of time and effort only ensures his appearing in an acceptable shirt chosen from the continually changing variety. In so far as a person's knowledge of the intrinsic qualities of a good, and of its fashion, is limited the growth of variety subjects him to some strain, and possibly to some anxiety.

he be coerced into a wiser course of action. Without taking issue with this doctrine as a political maxim it should none the less be transparent that in many circumstances some measure of constraint on a man's choice can increase his welfare. To illustrate with a homely example, the concept of 'consumer's rent' may be employed by the economist to measure the *additional* benefit a man enjoys in choosing to smoke two packets of cigarettes a day for the rest of his life compared with a situation in which, say, no tobacco at all were available. Any restraint imposed by government edict, or any shortage that reduced his ration – directly or through higher prices – below two packages must necessarily appear as a reduction in his welfare. Yet it is far from impossible that if there were a tobacco famine, or if he were conscripted into some task-force which was sent to a place where tobacco could not be had, the craving for the weed might vanish over time, and the man live to bless the event. He would continue his life in better health, and pocket, than before, and assert roundly that his welfare had been vastly improved by these initially frustrating circumstances. This kind of event may be discussed with a great deal of political sophistication, but whatever is concluded it cannot be denied that a welfare economics based exclusively on free choice within institutional constraints does not recognize the ample opportunities for increasing social welfare by initial departures from the free-choice path. If, for example, television or cinema audiences were deprived for a longish period of the shallow entertainment they have habitually succumbed to, many of them might be expected, after a period of tedium, to develop a taste for more sophisticated programmes, so that if the old shabby fare became available again it would be rejected out of hand.

A short visit to the US is enough to convince one that wealth, competition, and free institutions provide no safeguards against the prevalence of appalling standards not only of environment in city and suburb but also in journalism and broadcasting entertainment. The opportunities for increasing social welfare through raising standards of taste and appreciation are not easily to be tapped in a highly commercial society.

Such reflections do not necessarily strengthen the arguments for the institution of philsopher-kings or weaken the arguments for political liberty. But they do serve to reveal the bias of welfare prescriptions that would accept as ultimate data the apparent and existing choices of people as if such choices come into being independently of the economic system.

If private enterprise has the freedom to expand resources in influencing the tastes of the public in the interest of larger profits, and if so far it has on balance been successful in influencing them for the worse, there can be surely no objection to non-commercial attempts to influence them for the better. To put the matter more formally, subsidies to agencies that support the arts (beyond the support given by the market) are to be justified by the net social benefits above the costs of such activities. And the opportunity for net benefits of this sort exist wherever such agencies are able to help people to form those habits of taste and discrimination which increase the capacity for aesthetic experience and enjoyment. A prolonged campaign to raise the public's standards of taste would appear to be a far more efficacious way of promoting social welfare than the present unimaginative policy of straining away at 'real' output.[1]

III

A final weakness in the link between effective choice and welfare is revealed by consideration of what economists are wont to call 'the relative income hypothesis' – the hypothesis that what matters more to a person in a high consumption society is not his absolute real income, his command over material goods, but his position in the income structure of society. In its purest form, the thesis asserts that, given the choice, the high-consumption society citizen would choose, for example, a 5 per cent increase in his own income, all other incomes constant, to, say, a 25 per cent increase in his income as part of a 25 per cent increase in everybody's real income. The evidence in favour of the hypothesis in its purest form is not conclusive but it is far from being implausible, and in a more modified form it is hardly to be controverted.

Our satisfaction with many objects depends upon their publicly recognized scarcity irrespective of their utility to us. It is not difficult to imagine the gratification experienced by a person living in a country in which all the other inhabitants are aware of his being the sole possessor of a radio, hi-fi recorder, washing-machine and other durables. Nor is it difficult to imagine his great satisfaction, arising from the knowledge of his being the sole possessor of these things, melting away as they

[1]The criteria of good taste and bad does not, in this connection, pose any formidable problem. So much that is produced for public consumption is incontestably bad by any standards and some of it is excellent by most standards that the question of locating the boundary between the two need not bother us for a long time yet.

become common household appurtenances; indeed, of his gradual dis-satisfaction with them as he learns that his neighbours now possess far more advanced models than his own. However, the more truth there is in this relative income hypothesis – and one can hardly deny the in-creasing emphasis on status and income-position in the affluent society – the more futile as a means of increasing social welfare is the official policy of economic growth.

In sum, facile generalization about the connection between effective choice and welfare – as a necessary link between expanding output and expanding welfare – which serve to quieten doubts concerning the single-minded pursuit of economic growth, are here rejected. The fact that what matters most to affluent-society man is not the growth of his purchasing power *per se* but his relative status, his position in the income structure, robs the policy of industrial growth of much of its conventional economic rationale. In part at least, this attitude of affluent-society man is to be explained by the thesis developed in Parts II and III; that over the last two decades, at least, economic growth has failed to provide men with those choices that are really significant for raising welfare; indeed, that on balance social welfare is likely to have fallen inasmuch as the post-war industrial expansion has incidentally destroyed much of the cardinal sources of welfare hitherto available. The bewildering assort-ment of manufactures and fashion goods do not go far to compensate. It offers to men an expansion of choice that is as likely to subtract from than to add to his welfare.

As producer, affluent-society man has little choice but to adapt him-self to the prevailing technology. No provision is made by industry enabling him, if he chooses, to forgo something in the way of earnings for more creative and more enjoyable work. Nor, as citizen, has he yet been presented with the choice of quieter and more humane environ-ments, free of noise and motorized traffic.

Part V

Reflections on the Unmeasurable Consequences
of
Economic Growth

Chapter 14

Introduction

I

The clichès that come jingling towards the end of the company director's annual address about the company's unwavering belief in economic progress (to which the company makes a modest contribution) and its power to make the world a richer, more varied, and more 'exciting' place to live in, have already been subjected to some buffeting in the previous pages. What slender links remain between economic growth and social welfare must now come under further strain as we remove some of the pegs from the framework of analysis familiar to economists.

The old-fashioned economic law of eventually diminishing marginal utility was founded on the supposed satiation of human wants, whether the wants were physical, intellectual, aesthetic or emotional. No matter how rich he becomes a man has still but one pair of eyes, one pair of ears, one stomach, one sexual organ, a single brain and a single nervous system. In the face of this unremarkable fact of life, continuous material growth cannot be sustained by a system geared simply to producing ever larger quantities of the same goods. Hence the importance of product innovation. New and more expensive goods and services continuously supervene. And in the endeavour to ensure that men change their wants as rapidly, the economic system must be no less adept at creating dissatisfaction. Its success in this respect is symbolized by the post-war emergence of the 'pace-setter' – an ideal type, hyperconscious of being in the van of fashion, and imbued with the new virtues of 'dynamism', expertise and unlimited ambition. The more affluent a society the more covetous it needs to be. Keep a man covetous – 'achieve-ment-motivated' is the approved term – and, with the help of his wife and doctor, he may be kept running hard to the last day of his life.

But for what? Indeed, it is not so much the belief that there must be some hypothetical limit to a man's capacity for enjoyment that is at issue. I should imagine that man today is far removed from any such limit. What is pertinent, however, is whether by unabating pursuit of material growth he tends, on balance, to converge towards this limit or, on balance, to move away from it. And what is the evidence which suggests, say, that for today's *bon vivants* the experience of life as a whole is any richer than it was for yesterday's *bon vivants* – a sceptical view of things no less applicable to the future? That new opportunities, such as visiting the moon, exploring the oceans, travelling at unimaginable speeds, gazing at three-dimensional television screens, using visual telephonic communication, pressing buttons on miracle computers, raising of test-tube babies, and much more besides, will all be available to our grandchildren – if the world survives – need not be doubted. What is to be doubted surely is whether, after their novelty has worn off, the experience of these things can be counted on to deepen the enjoyment of life in comparison with the life people have been leading in different periods and in other civilizations.

Be that as it may, there is unmistakable evidence that much of the enjoyment of life still attainable is effectively marred by a chronic restlessness to realize that which is bigger and better. Though one may ride roughshod over a multitude of doubts to a brave tattoo on the theme of man's 'infinite adaptability', the fact remains that man's bodily chemistry, his basic instincts and emotional needs have not, as yet, been altered. Sheer force of will and intellect may, for a while, enable him to act so as to appear to be adapting himself to, and coping with, a physical environment that changes more rapidly each year, but there is much in the rest of his being that will continue – until science can alter it – to protest at the growing stresses to which it is subjected. Thousands of slaves were sacrificed in the building of the pyramids of Egypt. Today we are our own task-masters, dedicating our lives to erecting pyramids of material achievement. Immersed, as we are, in heaping Pelion on Ossa we pay no heed to the latent antagonisms between the demands of an advanced technological civilization and the demands of man's instinctual nature. In the ruthless transformation of our plant home – the only planet, incidentally, we can comfortably live on – we are concurrently destroying much that man's nature doted on in the past: a sense of intimately belonging, of being part of a community in which each man had his place;

a sense of being close to nature, of being close to the soil and to the beasts of the field that served him; a sense of being a part of the eternal and unhurried rhythm of life.

It would be as untrue to assert that in all past civilizations a feeling of security and contentment were experienced by all families as it would be idle to deny that many suffered from hardship, disease and poverty. But wherever people lived comfortably, whether in town or village, or farm, their satisfactions were rooted ultimately in their closeness to each other and to the natural order of their lives.

II

We shall not, however, pursue this train of thought here, since it is no part of our plan to reconstruct a faithful picture of the world we began to lose in the nineteenth century. Rather, we shall confine ourselves in the following pages to consider the ways in which the organized pursuit and realization of technological progress themselves act to destroy the chief ingredients that contribute to men's well-being.

This last sentence provides the justification for including the present section. The reflections, of their own, have no pretensions to novelty: reflections of a similar kind, though more subtly or more forcefully expressed, may be found in memoirs, novels, essays and in literary journals. Those elaborated here, however, claim to be directly relevant to the costs-of-growth thesis. Thus the suggestion merely that many of the less congenial aspects of life today are not just a passing phase, or an abnormal prolongation of some freak of fashion, is neither original nor interesting. To have any claim on our attentions such aspects must be fitted into the larger picture. Hence the attempt in the following pages to reveal a close connection between the many symptoms of social malaise and the processes generated by economic growth.

I must confess, however, to having failed to discover any central theme about which these less formal considerations might be made to cohere in some simple pattern. Sustained cogitation might eventually disclose one. In the meantime I have grouped the variety of considerations under several main headings and ordered them in roughly ascending importance – the remarks on cult of efficiency, which close Part IV, carrying the gravest implications for social welfare. The two chapters on profit-propelled growth form something of a digression. They discuss some of the disruptive developments brought about chiefly by commercial enterprise in a wealthy economy, developments that are not unavoidably associated with technological advance. For what the distinction is worth, they are not therefore so 'inevitable' as are the developments treated in the other chapters.

The question of inevitability requires, perhaps, a further word of explanation. The strictly pragmatic reader, patient enough with arguments critical of the present dispensation so long as alternative dispensations are shown to be available, many begin to demur as he reads on. Granted that on balance the unmeasurable consequences of economic growth are unfavourable to social welfare they are, apparently, inescapable. For better or worse we are wedded to technological advance. For all practical purpose it is 'built into' the system. Progress is compulsive, not deliberate.

Not all readers are pragmatists however. If the arguments are, in the main, valid the connections between economic growth and, for instance social disintegration is surely of interest to many people. Moreover, if the public is eventually convinced of these connections, its response need not be ineffectual. At least disappointments are avoided if it remains sceptical of measures undertaken to accelerate the creation of material wealth. More important, people could conceivably reject the conscious pursuit of economic growth as a prime end of economic policy. They could turn from the clamour for more science and more industrial investment, and begin to think instead of specific proposals for adding a margin of ease and pleasantness to their brief sojourn on this earth.

III

In so far as an excursion into the non-measurable consequences of economic growth entail selective comparisons between past and present, a postscript is called for. The question, which age offered to ordinary men and women a greater sense of fulfilment, though difficult to determine, is not meaningless. It may well be dismissed, however, by those subscribing to a historical relativism which demands that the record of any historical period be judged only in relation to the beliefs, practices, and institutions of that period. Pursued to its logical conclusion, such a thesis implies that no period in history be judged virtuous and none iniquitous. The attempt to withhold value judgements on the past makes commentary, even description, difficult. More important, unless we believe that there are ingredients essential to the good life, and unless we can agree on a definition of civilized living, which enables us to pass judgement on past, present and future, we have no lights by which to guide our own destiny. Society may believe it is able to choose, but if the consequences of one choice rather than another cannot be evaluated in terms of better or worse there can be no incentive to establish a more effective machinery of social choice.

If, on the other hand, the possibility of judgement is admitted, both moral judgement about the behaviour of people and factual judgement about their sense of well-being, we must proceed cautiously. Every age has a tendency to interpret history in the light of its own institutions, its own achievements, its own ideology, if only because time is uni-directional: all past history is seen by any age as leading up to the age in question. And while hindsight reveals to us the follies of our ancestors, we must depend upon humility to persuade ourselves that our behaviour is no less irrational and hypocritical than theirs seems to us. The pro-fessional historian, with a disciplined imagination, has difficulties enough in appreciating how people actually felt about the things they said and did. One can expect less of the ordinary reader of history who can hardly help being misled by the propensity of the modern author, eager to engage the interests of a wide public by making history 'come alive', to reinterpret the past using the idiom, the metaphors, the psychology and the analogies of the present.

Of course, a man may be an incurable optimist holding to the doctrine of social evolution as an article of faith. In the presence of such a man it is not possible to single out any favourable feature of a bygone age without, at least eliciting a charge of romanticizing the past and, as likely as not, eliciting also a sardonic reminder of the statistics bearing on poverty and infantile mortality.[1] In fact it is much easier to fall into the

[1] There is another view about mortality statistics however. According to E. F. Schumacher ('Clean Air and Future Energy', *Des Voeux Memorial Lecture*, October 1967): The US Public Health Service states that 'About 40·9 per cent of persons living in the US were reported to have one or more chronic conditions. While some of these conditions were relatively minor, others were serious con-ditions such as heart disease, diabetes, or mental illness.' . . . Even the achieve-ments in prolonging life are not impressive except for the very young. In America, the life expectancy of a white male aged forty-five years has increased by only 2·9 years since 1900, and that of a sixty-five-year-old man by only 1·2 years . . . At the same time, the expenditure on medical services in the US now amounts to some $50, billion a year, or about *five dollars a week* for every man, woman, and child, on average.

According to Lewis Herber (*Our Synthetic Environment*, London, 1963): 'Many individuals seem to be succumbing to degenerative diseases long before

opposite error of romanticizing the future and presenting too gloomy a picture of the past.[1] The evolutionist in particular is prone to reach general conclusions about the quality of life in some past epoch by inter-temporal comparisons based on those features of life on which the present, not the past, lays the greatest emphasis – features that are, indeed, sometimes outside the range of experience and expectations of our forbears – rising material standards, for instance, or hygiene, or glamour, or social mobility, or physical passivity, or speed of travel. Again, looking beyond the 'industrial revolution' (which was, by almost any standards, one of the worst times in history for the working classes), and contemplating the long hours of physical toil endured by the humbler folk (at certain times of the year) during earlier periods the modern man may well be appalled. For he lives in a society that is straining ingenuity to enter the millennium of effortless living.

Yet there is little evidence that among the working classes hard physical work, as such, was resented. Provided land was plentiful relative to population, vast inequalities of wealth and station, intolerable to the modern mind, were accepted as part of the eternal nature of things. A man today must be narrowly attuned to the times if he cannot conceive that an unquestioned acceptance of one's place in the social hierarchy may be more conducive to a carefree spirit than the obsessive struggle for status in a rapidly changing economy.

And if the evolutionist is apt to err in comparing the experience of life in past ages by reference to the values of the present, in comparing the expected future with the present he takes no care to be at least consistent in error. Faced with some of the seemingly less attractive features of life to be expected at some point of time, say, within the next hundred years – a world population ten times that of the present; megapolitan urban clusters of between twenty and fifty million inhabitants; the universal employment of robots or some science-created

they reach the prime of life. Not only is cancer a leading cause of death in childhood and youth, but . . . many American males between twenty and thirty years of age are on the brink of a major cardiac disease . . . If diseases of this kind represent the normal deterioration of the body, then human biology is taking a patently abnormal turn. A large number of people are breaking down prematurely.'

[1] Even if there were, on balance, a presumption in favour of life in the present, it would be proper in this essay to draw attention to some of the more vital aspects of the older societies that have crumbled before the tide of advancing technology.

species of sub-human to cater to our physical comforts; the disappearance of agriculture and the production instead of synthetic foods by electro-chemical processes; an establishment served by giant computers to direct and record our movements in all detail; control of the weather; a sky never free of flying objects; the obsolescence of language and the demise of society – the evolutionist will either exorcize them with the magic word 'challenge' or else, in an excess of philosophy, surmise that at such a future time people will have fully adapted themselves to such conditions. They will have accepted them as in every way natural – a concession he does not, of course, extend to the conditions existing in 'the bad old days'.[1]

IV

In short, the method of argument espoused by those who pin their faith in progress is, on the one hand, to affirm the greater richness of life in the foreseeable future by selecting the technically 'exciting' features while rationalizing the repellent ones by reference to man's infinite capacity for adaptation (in witness thereof, people's successful adaptation to the rapidly changing world of today): on the other hand, to affirm the harshness of life in ages past by ignoring the natural and spiritual sources of satisfaction and dwelling, instead, on the record of physical hardship endured by the labouring masses – anathema to an age devoted to extirpating effort from the routine of living – and of the barbarities and dangers which in fact differ from those besetting our own day and age only in being less familiar to us.

Yet, if by Divine interposition, a sixteenth-century yeoman, say, were enabled to read through the newspapers of the last fifty years, what

[1]The evolutionist is prone to other asymmetries in argument. Going back over the centuries he is sure to find men of each epoch declaring the superiority of their day and age to all preceding periods, and expecting greater things from the future. Utterances such as these are accepted as solid evidence of progress. In contrast, the observations of men who throughout history have deferred to a previous age, and who with sorrow have remarked the disappearance of the commons, the vanishing countryside, the spread of commercial greed and industrialization, are never accepted as evidence of a worsening of conditions, but as clear evidence of men's illusions.

In defence of social evolution there are always the mortality figures and productivity statistics to draw upon. Whereas any mention of the unhappier features of modern life is countered by quoting from the 'Jeremiahs' of previous ages. Things never change for the worse: in that respect, *plus ça change plus c'est la même chose.*

would he think of the casualties inflicted in two world wars, and a score of others also? Would he compare the Gestapo favourable with the Inquisition? Confining ourselves to 'peacetime', would he envy the numbers of people today all vainly trying to find a quiet place to live? What would he think of the time it takes to get to work and back each day? What would he think of the unquestioned belief that life should be spent scrambling to keep ahead? What would be his response to newspaper reports of sex maniacs, arson, drug addiction among the young, increasing juvenile violence and race riots? Or of the hundred thousand killed and maimed each year by their own countrymen in pursuit of the pleasures of private motoring? Would he not shudder at what he read, and seek to influence the Almighty by prayers and fasting to spare his descendants from a fate so vile?

Chapter 15

The Growing Menace of Obsolescence

I

The appearance in history of mercantile societies is associated in the popular mind with the growth of the arts, philosophy and literature. Yet only with the advent of modern industrial societies does it become possible to offer to all men those material and educational opportunities undreamed of in pre-industrial civilizations. The path of progress has not always been smooth, however, and modern history books are seldom at a loss for examples of benighted resistance to technological innovations by ordinary people apparently deficient in historical vision. Indeed, any number of economists can testify today to uphill struggles undergone to induce native populations in economically backward regions to forsake the methods of their forefathers and to come to terms with the notion of efficiency. For one of the prerequisites for the so-phrased 'take-off into self-sustained economic growth' is the collapse of traditional values and the growth of dissatisfaction with the *status quo*.

In so far as the traditional mode of life was indeed deficient in variety and opportunity, dissatisfaction with it is not to be deprecated. What the modern world tends to forget, however, is that dissatisfaction with existing circumstances too easily becomes a habit of mind – a by-product of the commercial society that brought it into being and a condition for the advancement of that kind of society. Bernard Shaw put it succinctly in calling discontent the mainspring of progress. And if, as so many of us seem to believe, progress is to be regarded as *the* social priority then such costs as are incurred in its promotion are incidental and secondary in importance. Even if some of the unhappy consequences are all too evident their imponderable nature tells against them. After all, this is a scientific age, and what cannot be measured need not be reckoned with.

Notwithstanding such modern prejudice, let us fasten our attention on considerations, too easily brushed aside, that are closely connected with the phenomenon of unabating material progress. First, that it is hardly possible to move along this golden path of self-perpetuating economic growth without subjecting people to manifold pressures, pressures that appear to increase both with the stage of economic growth and with the rate of economic growth. While it is true that a great deal of anxiety about the morrow was prevalent in previous ages – and for many good reasons; fear of famine, of plague or of unemployment – it is less excusable in the wealthy societies of today in which (excepting the hard core of poverty) material well-being and medical attention are assured for the mass of the people. For all that, whether viewed as producer or consumer or social being, few men today can say that they live, in this age of accelerating change, without any awareness of anxiety.

The status, if not the earnings, of the professional man, the scientist or the university don, has never been higher. To all appearances, his position is comfortable and secure. Yet today he has to keep up with a quite unprecedented flow of highly technical literature in his field of endeavour. He may, especially if young and impressionable, react to this sort of strain by talking about the 'exhilaration of modern life' or the 'challenge of living in an age of continuous change', but unless he is outstandingly gifted, he has no certainty from one year to the next of being able to cope with technical developments that come at him thick and fast. If the pace is not too gruelling this year, it may well be so next year, or the year after that. The penalty of slipping behind, or of falling out of the race, may be the forfeit of all that he has struggled to achieve and to hold on to in a competitive society – prestige, position, the recognition and companionship of colleagues; the things that buoy him up in an ocean of anonymity.

For the workman, skilled or otherwise, the pressure to keep abreast of technical developments may be slight in comparison but his anxiety is also provided for. Gone are the days when a man, qualified to be a master of his craft, ceased his climbing, stepped on to the plateau, his place recognized and secure in the community he served. There were trials a'plenty in a man's life, but there was not the fear that any year might see him undone and the skills by which he lived, the source of his pride and satisfaction, fall into desuetude. With the trend, however, towards rapid changes of demand, and, more important, rapid industrial innovation, it needs more than the power of his union, more even than the power of the welfare state, to afford a workman any assurance about his future. Skills painstakingly acquired over many years may become obsolete in as many months. And it is not earnings alone that matter to a man. High unemployment pay and re-training opportunities do not suffice to compensate him for losing his position in the hierarchy of his chosen occupation, for seeing his hard-earned skill and experience thrown on the mounting scrap-heap of obsolete tools.

Since change today is faster and more thorough than it was, say, a generation ago, and a generation hence will be faster yet, every one of us, manager, workman or scientist, lives closer to the brink of obsolescence. Each one of us that is adult and qualified feels menaced in some degree by the push of new developments which establish themselves only by discarding the methods and techniques and theories that he has learned to master.

The same influence operates on a person regarded as a member of the family. Today's young people, those under thirty say, being breathless in pursuit of life-experience and opportunities for status-training are not acutely aware of any hiatus in their lives left by the disintegration of communities, once centred about church and temple, through which people of all ages and circumstances organized their social activities and became familiar with one another. This lack of a social community will, however, be felt as they move into their later years. Inasmuch as experience counts for less and knowledge, up-to-date knowledge, for more in a world of recurring obsolescence, the status of older men falls relative to that of younger men. And within the family the same force is at work. There was a time, not long ago, when grandparents were, as a matter of course, part of the family circle, and not necessarily an impediment to its activities. Being full of years gave them the right to be heard in virtue of long experience of the ways of the world: the young of all ages might turn to them for counsel, sympathy and affection. The rapidity of change in social conventions and moral attitudes, associated with the technological transformation in the mode of living, renders a person's experience of the world a generation ago largely irrelevant to the problems of the young today. Never was there such a time when grandparents felt quite so useless and unwanted.[1]

---

[1] In this pace-making technological civilization the practice is to shunt old people, like obsolete machines, out of the way of today's smaller and more mobile families. And though some of the old are fortunate enough not to have

Finally, as a consumer, a person's welfare can be adversely affected by continuous product innovation. To have to choose from an ever-swelling variety of products, made possible by intensive advertising, whose comparative qualities and performances are, for the most part, beyond our powers to appraise, can be a tiresome and worrying business. Current analyses of the relative importance of the informative, entertainment, and persuasive elements in any type of advertisement, or statistics of the average degree of success of advertising campaigns, are of little relevance here. It may well be true that few people are actually cajoled or frightened into buying things they do not want, though it may also be true that the very ubiquity and near unavoidability, of modern advertising, can jar and exasperate. Far more important, however, is its over-all influence as an integral institution of the economies of the West. Living in a world saturated with advertisements may well make a man cynical enough to resist the most persuasive selling technique. But though he successfully ignores the message of each and every advertisement, their cumulative effect over time in teasing his sense and tapping repeatedly at his greeds, his vanity, his lusts and ambitions, can hardly leave his character unaffected. Again, by drawing his attention daily to the mundane and material, by hinting continually that the big prizes in life are the things that only money can buy, the influences of advertising and popular journalism conspire to leave a man restless and discontented with his lot. These influences, moreover, are rapidly producing a society in which standards of taste and of decorum are in a continuous state of obsolescence, leaving fashion alone as the arbiter of moral behaviour.

II

Once we take economic growth to encompass not merely the growth of material goods and services, but the growth also of all the social consequences entailed in rapid technological advance – both the proliferation of disamenities which, as argued, might be mitigated by saner

---

to depend upon their pensions for their material wants, they perforce must suffer emotional deprivation. The growth in separate provision of old people's homes, and old people's flats and villages (considerately furnished with gadgets enabling the infirm to keep house without the help of the young and able), which promotes their isolation from the rest of society – where they are entertained from time to time by social workers and, somehow, jollied along to the grave – may well be the most efficient way of disposing of them. The least that can be said of this form of social vivisection is that it adds to the anxieties of growing old.

institutions, and the less tangible though, perhaps, more potent effects that impair our capacity to enjoy life – there is little one can salvage from the exhilarating vision of sustained economic growth that is suggestive of net social advantage. It might seem reasonable to suppose that although so much expenditure of time and resource goes to producing gadgetry, the small expenditure devoted to cultural subjects is not insignificant when measured in absolute terms. Yet in the atmosphere created by rapid economic growth, an atmosphere in which the 'new' and the 'different' appear as the ultimate criteria, even statistics of cultural advance are suspect.

We are told, for example, that out of the 85 million records sold in Britain in 1964, 12 million were of classical music. These figures will almost certainly rise in the near future, but one would be hard-pressed to elicit them as evidence of a cultural renaissance. Any multiplication of this number is obviously consistent with a general picture of a society of determined 'pace-setters'. What surely is relevant are the dominant motives of the record-collectors. And here one cannot lightly dismiss the notion that classical records are for many people tokens of taste and objects of display. It is possible that collectors play their records frequently but with an enjoyment somewhat alloyed by a concern with current vogues in music and sometimes marred by too determined a desire to acquire a musical vocabulary.

Sustained economic growth, at least in the richer communities, depends heavily on an atmosphere of being 'with it', and though not all 'with it' ambitions are unworthy, the more secondary is the purely aesthetic motivation the less intrinsically rewarding is the cultural pursuit in question, whether it be listening to music, visiting art galleries or attending operas. True, one does not have to wait the arrival of the twentieth century to find people attending cultural functions purely for reasons of fashion or in order to diversify their repertoire. Novelists throughout the centuries have made merry with such stock characters. But this is neither here nor there in so far as the interpretation of current statistics is at issue. One may safely conjecture that along with the present confused interest in adult education, 'culture', in small packages at least, happens to be currently in fashion. And the swelling sales figures of publishers and record companies are less plausibly interpreted as a mass renaissance and more plausibly interpreted as yet another manifestation of the growing affluence of young 'status-seekers'.

III

The effects of the post-war spread of television is relevant in this connection. Though occasionally it is agreed that television has destroyed
much of the intimacy of family life by funnelling into the privacy of the
home the raucous distractions and paraphernalia of other worlds, real
and imaginary, it is held, at best, to be potentially an educative force
of immense efficacy. The topics discussed by panels of speakers cover
morals, politics, science, crime, economics, sex, history, art, music and
bringing-up-the-children, so enabling the alert public to appreciate all
sides of a question. If people do not acquire encyclopedic knowledge –
and most of them have forgotten by Thursday what they thought they
had learned on the Wednesday – they at least acquire an increasing
measure of tolerance. Such tolerance, however, is borne less of enlightenment as of uncertainty and bewilderment. The repeated re-examinations,
for instance, of fundamental questions about religion, ethics, crime,
etcetera, with their unavoidable inconclusiveness, serve further to weaken
the moral props of an already disintegrating society and to destroy a
belief in divinity that once gave hope and comfort to many. The distinctions between good and bad, between right and wrong, between
virtue and vice, once held to be self-evident by our forebears, are blurred
and reblurred. In consequence, the confidence of ordinary men and
women both in their opinions and in their judgements is gradually
being eroded, and along with it their self-respect and essential dignity.

What is more, this rapid extension of specialized opinion to every
aspect of knowledge and daily living acts to inhibit the spontaneity of a
man's thought and expression. Where a century or two ago the ordinary
civilized man would speculate boldly on any subject and converse
joyfully on all manner of topics, his spirit today is muted in dismal
deference to the cumulative discoveries of science and the qualified
pronoucements of the experts. His personality shrivels. He has no
convictions to sustain him. His discourse perforce becomes restricted
to jest, trivial observations and personal reminiscence.[1]

[1] Once one accepts the fact of an advanced technological society, in which
television is the popular medium of entertainment and information, any recom-
mendation that certain programmes be discontinued invites the charge of being
an enemy of 'The Open Society'. But if one is condemned, one need not remain
silent. In so far as liberty is deemed extended as a larger number of people
hear a greater variety of views, the only conclusion that follows from the above
remarks is that, if true, there can be circumstances in which considerations of
social welfare and of liberty pull in opposite directions.

Chapter 16

Our Shrinking Planet

I

We do not need the oil companies' advertisements to inspire us to become 'get-away people'. With the unchecked deterioration of environment in town, city, and suburb, get-away people are being provided with more and more to get away from. But where to? When millions are on the move to get away it is unlikely that many will succeed.

One of the paradoxes of our time is that while language is used increasingly to promote expectations of a continuing enlargement of vista – in post-war journalese all discernible possibilities are 'new and exciting', all opportunities are 'rapidly expanding', and life itself is being mercilessly 'enriched' with 'new dimensions of experience'. Speed barriers, sex barriers, *xyz* barriers are about to be 'crashed', and scientific 'breakthroughs' occur about once a week – there is ample evidence that men are beginning to suffer from a sense of claustrophobia.

An obvious cause of this growing sense of claustrophobia is the rapid development of communications, in particular the continually publicized endeavours to increase the speed of travel. Having succeeded already in moving people through the air at a speed exceeding that of sound, the spirit of progress demands that there be no slackening in man's efforts to bring forward the day when we shall sail through space at a speed no less than that of light itself. If it should take us but an hour to reach Hong Kong from London, a further reduction of the journey-time to a half-hour would unquestionably be accepted as an improvement. Yet one of the more manifest and lamentable, consequences of bringing places ever closer together in time is that this earth, once thought immense, now seems dwarf-sized. Not so long ago, even a few years after the turn of the century, the world was still a spacious place, a world of vast oceans and continents. Today one has to return to the sea stories of Melville or Conrad to recapture the image of a measureless ocean on which seamen ventured. One could once speak with awe of far-away places reached only by perilous sea voyages stretching over weeks or months; one could speak of distant lands unknown to men, of uncharted seas, of impassable mountain ranges, of fearsome and savage jungles, of coral islands in the South Seas, and enchanting islanders far removed from the corruption of white civilization, of an Africa teeming with wild life and warlike tribes, and of quaint and colourful customs in distant lands as yet unspoiled by modern commerce. True, unless one were a sailor or in very comfortable circumstances, one might never venture beyond the British coast. But for everyone there was still this sense of living in a world of uncountable resources, climates, and peoples, a world of inexhausible variety and strangeness and colour. Even if most people could only read about, and dream about, sailing off to distant shores, they could yet be hugely fascinated by the tales of travellers returning from places no farther than Switzerland or Spain.

Today, no country is more than a few hours away by plane, and the years will see these few hours whittled down to minutes. Not only will the earth appear to our children as a pitifully tiny affair, it will also appear irredeemably monotonous – so much so, perhaps, that they will seek relief flying through the frozen darkness of space and groping their way over dead planets. We have already spoken of the phenomenal growth of tourism as the most potent factor in the destruction of the earth's dwindling resources of natural beauty. In the attempt to cater for the growing millions of tourists by building hotels, villas, lidos, arcades, casinos, roads, airfields, once dreamy resorts and semi-tropical islands are transmogrified into neon-lit Meccas, agape with jostling crowds and swarming with transistorized automobiles. Any hope of escape far from the madding crowd is, for each of us, flickering out.[1]

[1] At the same time, and in the sacred name of economic efficiency, one of the few peaceful prospects that men still enjoy once the suburbs are behind them, a scene at once familiar, picturesque and reassuring, that of cattle grazing on hill, dale and pastureland, is disappearing. As scientists discover new chemicals, a growing proportion of our livestock will never set foot on soil, but will be herded instead into animal factories, there to be blown up to a size and transmuted to a precise texture as quickly and cheaply as is technologically feasible – little thought being spared by the commercial interests involved to the mute sufferings of these helpless creatures.

And it is not merely the case that our planet is dwindling in size, the differences between places are dwindling also. The annihilation of distance is accompanied by the annihilation of variety. The differences in manners, in customs, in cultures, clothes, food, architecture, differences that once made travel so fascinating an experience are rapidly being extinguished. Fashions in clothes, pop-music, architecture, are becoming increasingly international. Fifty years ago, no more, there were still striking differences between localities in Britain, as much with respect to building as to dialect. Today, one could choose dozens of these new makeshift office blocks to be found in London, or in any other large city, which are in no visible respect any different from their counterparts in other cities from Buenos Aires to Detroit, and from Sidney to Dusseldorf. Of course, there are sporadic efforts to encourage local costumes, music and handicrafts, sometimes for cultural or nostalgic reasons, but more often with a view to encouraging tourist dollars to flow in the required direction. Notwithstanding which the consummation of this trend in a uniform cosmopolitanism can hardly be far off.

II

One must add to the annihilation of distance and the consequent destruction of variety, the annihilation of time; for a related effect of economic growth, and the atmosphere in which it flourishes, is the psychological imbalance between present and future. Economic growth promotes a predominantly 'forward-looking' spirit, one well illustrated by the automobile and oil advertisements with their steely-eyed young executives gazing unflinchingly into the empyrean. Surely no other period in history can have produced perorations laden with such solemnity as 'the future of our children', 'the future of our people', 'the future of the nation', 'the future of our science', 'the future of the free world', 'the future of mankind'. By contrast with this habitual concern with the future, any thought to the present for its own sake must seem improvident, if not vulgar. The more we are conditioned by the Press, by modern business, by scientists, to think in terms of the future, the more indifferent we become to the ugliness spreading about us. The more pie there is in the sky to gaze at, the less attention we pay to what is happening here, on this earth, right now. If we are daily assaulted by the noise of motorized traffic, the perpetual drilling and dust of demolition, we can always turn to the rising statistics of production for consolation.

This fixation on the future enters our lives and affects our well-being in more ways than one. Each of us, in his own affairs, accepts it as the hallmark of prudence to be ever planning for the future, whether we are hoarding money or expertise, building goodwill, seeking promotion, or anticipating a vacation (all too often for the express purpose of restoring our health to enable us to return and perform our daily tasks with renewed efficiency). Our eyes are ever on the clock and our calendars marked for weeks and months ahead. Today's news is barely read before we are impatient of tomorrow's. The very focus of our experience runs ahead of us. The current of events, here and now, passes through us but faintly, so pre-empted are our minds with matters to come.

Thus, the pure taste of the present eludes us. For in this world that we are intent on changing as rapidly as we can, the material advantages are to be reaped by those who look farthest ahead – those who treat the receding present as a jumping-off ground for the future. But this 'futurism', this greed for the rewards of the future, this impatience to realize the shape of things to come, which inspires and fuels the present technological revolution, is just the phenomenon that hastens us through our brief lives and effectively cheats us of all sense of the spaciousness of time. Today the art of immersing oneself wholly in the stream of the present is known only to children, and to people living in more settled and traditional societies.

Chapter 17

Salvation by Science: 1

I

The image of scientists as a fraternity dedicated to the pursuit of knowledge for the ultimate benefit of humanity is a comforting one. Many a popular book on the scientists of yesterday and today present a picture of men of vision struggling against the prejudices of the age, men from whose inspired theorizing and patient probings into the nature of the universe will come an age of greater glory for mankind. The names of Newton, Pasteur, Mme Curie, Darwin, Einstein, have powerful associations. Not only are they dedicated beings, they are good people, uninterested in the wordly things except for their concern with humanity. They are seen, in fact, as having all the attributes of a priesthood: great esoteric knowledge, immunity from wordly temptations, faith in mankind and prophetic vision.

This popular impression, however, does not stand up to scrutiny. Collective knowledge does indeed continue to grow in extent and complexity, but increasingly it is scattered among the growing army of the learned. In the past, when the world moved at a more leisurely pace and the sum of man's knowledge was substantially smaller, scientists were few in number and their qualifications sprang from genius rather than from arduous or specialized training. Of the scores of thousands of scientists to be found today in all the richer countries only a small proportion can be sufficiently gifted to keep in advance of developments along a broad front of knowledge without strain. For a large number of the fraternity, however, there is nothing for it but to plod along fired by hope or compelled by anxiety. Whether young or old, whether employed in institutes, research establishments, or universities, all today are subject to a growing pressure on their time and on their innate capacity in consequence of the sheer output of current research, theoretical and applied. Not only must the scientist strive to keep abreast of the avalanche of journal literature, in which, inevitably, the writing is increasingly concentrated and increasingly technical. If he is ever to achieve some modicum of recognition he must himself contribute a learned paper from time to time to the accumulating weight that is bearing down on him. Thus, more than other professions, perhaps, the ordinary academic tends to become over-extended, his faculties too polarized to respond fully to other aspects of life, be they intellectual, aesthetic or emotional. Like all too many of us today, he may seek gaiety but is hard put to generate any.

One need not wonder long about how a person of modest abilities becomes a scientist, or a university teacher, at a time when the sum of knowledge is growing apace and at a time when the standards of scholarship are undeniably higher than ever they were. Two factors have made this possible: one is the longer period of training during which the ambitious student tends to neglect all but the minimum of social activity. Indeed, few students come to the frontiers of their speciality before the age of twenty-five and some not before thirty – their more creative years, perhaps, behind them. The other factor is the trend towards specialization. With the increase in numbers working in his chosen field, the specialist sooner or later feels the pinch. Sooner or later his response will be to hive off a smaller segment of the field and devote himself to its more intense cultivation. Close to the frontiers of any subject we shall find thousands of ordinary but hard-working people, each assiduously sifting his own thimbleful of earth.

This continual splitting and re-splitting of the subject, by which process a myriad of workers may be eventually accommodated over the whole spectrum of any academic discipline, has the unsurprising consequence that only a handful of men know well more than a fraction of the broader discipline in which they work, or are competent to judge the work of their colleagues over a wide field. Editors of learned journals already have difficulties in finding scholars able to appraise the quality of some of the highly specialized papers submitted to them. The postwar trend towards learned papers authored by two, three, four or more names bears further testimony to the growth of specialization and to the difficulties of keeping abreast of the literature in closely related fields. Indeed, such are the demands upon his time and capacity that no scholar is able to read more than a fraction of the output of professional papers in his own field. To quote an estimate made by Professor John Wilkinson, the average scientific paper is read by about 1.3 people – while many are read by several people and a few by hundreds, a large number are read by nobody but their authors (if we exclude the editors).[1] One may well wonder what the situation will be like a generation hence. That our form of civilization will eventually collapse under the weight of the unco-ordinated knowledge that is growing, in impressionistic terms, at an exponential rate, is not so unreasonable a hypothesis.[2]

II

Nor does the picture of scientists as a group immune from worldly temptations bear looking at too closely. There is no reason why science and learning should appeal only to the pure in mind and motive. Its prestige has never stood higher – nothing could be more 'in' than science. On the more successful of its devotees it confers not only status but substantial material rewards: even those of modest talents may have profitable associations with government and industry. In the event, scientists have been drawn into the unending scramble for material rewards and public recognition, along with business executives, actors and politicians. A man may be petty, vicious, coarse-grained, paranoid even, and, outside his specialism, thoroughly ignorant, and yet do well enough as a scientist or scholar. He may write a paper because of the intrinsic interest of the problem – indeed, some scientists become so absorbed in problem-solving as to ignore relevance completely – but he is not less likely than any other mortal to become interested in a study that carries with it some sizeable stipend or research grant. Moreover, whatever aspect of a subject engages his attention, he will be spurred on by the desire to 'get a paper out of it'; for the scientist counts his published works as a miser counts his gold. They are his kudos, his claims to

[1] John Wilkinson, 'The Quantitative Society, or What are you to do with Noodle', Occasional Paper published by the Center for the Study of Democratic Institutions, USA.

[2] What hopes there are for preventing further excessive fragmentation in any discipline would seem to rest partly on increased intellectual assistance from more highly developed computers, and partly on the possibilities of enlarging man's capacities. Chemical means of improving mental performance are in the experimental stage. Advances in genetics may soon enable us to produce super-brain humans.

recognition. Above all, they are his certificates encashable in the world he moves in.

These observations serve to adumbrate the pedestrian reality behind the glossy captions about 'science in the service of mankind' which herald a prospect of illimitable human benefit from scientific progress. Such captions do, however, express the common faith, a faith shared, needless to say, by the scientist himself. Indeed, the scientist will seldom question the effects, immediate or remote, of his contribution to human welfare. He may assert that increased knowledge of any sort is its own justification. But he is more likely to accept as a self-evident proposition that any addition to knowledge entails an extension of man's power over the universe, an extension of choice and, therefore, an improvement of his lot on earth. And should man not be made happier thereby, should he destroy himself in a nuclear war or corrupt himself utterly, then this surely is the fault of society, not of the scientists – a rather forlorn dichotomy since the scientist no less than the layman is the victim of the mis-use of science. Indeed, the response of the scientist to any failure or mis-application of science is the by-now familiar one of urging the application of yet more science. If the use in agriculture of certain chemical discoveries is found to have wiped out several species of beings, or to have caused some significant upset in the ecological equilibrium of a region, the scientist can be counted on to remark that more research is imperative. If men and women become increasingly maladjusted in this rapidly changing world of ours, this again calls for more research. Psychologists, neurologists, sociologists, sexologists, will be eager to diagnose these new and fascinating infirmities, themselves the product of technology that threatens to stifle society. The more calamitous the consequences, the greater the challenge. An uncertain picture emerges of applied science carefully sewing us up in some places while accidentally ripping us apart in others.

III

The innocent layman surrounded by a growing array of specialists of all kinds – in the social sciences by economists, sociologists, anthropologists, psychologists and others – is deluded into believing that his welfare is in good hands whereas, in fact, there is no social science expressly concerned with human welfare in the round. In any case, practitioners are increasingly emphasizing 'positive' as against 'normative' treatment in the development of the social sciences; they are concerned, that is, with hypotheses of existing relationships and not with prescription.

The social scientist is, apparently, a helpless spectator to continued social developments that are fraught with welfare implications. For man's experience of welfare is only to a limited extent influenced by the range of goods placed at his disposal by the economy. The more pervasive influences on his welfare arise from the existing technological conditions. These affect him directly in his capacity as productive agent responding passively to the evolving machinery of industry. They affect him indirectly, though crucially, by their ultimate determination of the matrix of society – by their impress on the shape of the environment, material, institutional and psychological, which constrains his personality.

But the technological conditions of production are not chosen with a view to enhancing man's experience of life. Nor has any social science the least say in their determination. They evolve solely in response to the requirements of industrial efficiency. Thus, the predominant influences bearing on man's welfare are generated accidentally; simply as a by-product of technological advance. It may well be suspected that the human frame and the human psyche are ill-adjusted to the style of living that technology is thrusting upon us, but willy-nilly technology marches on, leaving to the medical profession the unenviable task of dealing with an increasing number of casualties that are unable to cope with the strains and stresses of a rapidly changing world.

In one respect, at least, modern technology could hardly be more ingeniously fashioned than it is for depriving men of the exercise of their character as men. From the beginnings of the 'industrial revolution' men have become progressively more specialized in a narrow range of tasks whether they work in an office, factory or laboratory. Whatever the particular skill employed, all the other qualities of a man, important enough in earlier times – qualities like courage, loyalty, perseverance, integrity, resourcefulness, atrributes that once entered heavily into his future and into the esteem in which he was held – have begun to lose their value in this unheroic push-button age. In the serious business of earning a living, the other parts of men count for very little.

If he were born today, a Robin Hood, a Buffalo Bill, a Clive of India, a Lawrence of Arabia, would probably be a nonentity. There must be, living among us now, tens of thousands of men who in bygone ages would have been glad to venture forth across the oceans, to fight their way through forests, to push back frontiers and to found colonies and settlements, men who in the daily toil and hazard would discover comradeship and vindicate their manhood. Today they must perforce lead obscure and sedentary lives far removed from the restless force of nature, slumped in anonymity, imbibing synthetic visions from the meretricious flicker of a television screen.

Only so little ago as the last war, there were times when the man in uniform could sense the desperate drama in which he was involved. It was possible for people to believe, as they did believe, that the outcome of the struggle depended upon the mettle and morale of their countrymen, whether serving in the forces or in the home front. Men undistinguished in the ordinary business of life learned to live together in mutual tolerance and good humour while subject to a common discipline and to common dangers and deprivations. The friendships that arose in these circumstances were carefree, intimate, and enduring; rare enough in the organized self-seeking of the modern world and hardly to be thought of in the automated civilization of tomorrow. Whatever the toll in the tragedy, whatever the loss of treasure, the poignant and the heroic could not be denied either. But the Second World War is surely the last of the great wars whose outcome will depend upon mass participation. Though for the time being Western countries continue to finance armies of highly-trained men, useful enough at present for police action in some underdeveloped areas, the determining factor no longer lies in the qualities of those who man the guns. The scientist has unavoidably usurped the place and the prestige of the soldier. A push-button war may or may not be in the offing. But if such a war does come, the measure of its horror will reside in the manifest helplessness and uselessness of ordinary men of all ages. Those that die will not be killed in conventional enemy attacks but will be annihilated by the latest products of scientific achievement. They will not die in the battlefield but like rats in a trap.

Chapter 18

Salvation by Science: 2

I

Notwithstanding occasional declarations about its unlimited potentialities for social betterment science is not guided by any social purpose. As with technology, the effects on humanity are simply the by-products of its own self-seeking. As a collective enterprise, science has no more social conscience then the problem-solving computers it employs. Indeed, like some ponderous multi-purpose robot that is powered by its own insatiable curiosity, science lurches onward irresistibly, its myriad feelers peeling away the flesh of nature, probing ever deeper beneath the surface of things, forcing entry into every sanctuary, moving a transmuted humanity forward to the day when every throb in the universe has been charted, every manifestation of life dissected to the nth particle, and nothing more remains to be discovered – except, perhaps, the road back.

Long before that final consummation, however, we shall learn, too late, that men live not by truth alone, but by myth. Already science has stripped men of the comfort of their most cherished illusions; of the uniqueness of the earth they inhabit, placed in the centre of God's universe; of the immortality of their souls; of the assurance of paradise and life everlasting. In the place of myth, the heroic truths of Science: that man dwells on a small planet lit by an insignificant star somewhere near the rim of an immense galaxy in one of the countless number of galaxy systems scattered through the infinitudes of space; that far from being created in the image of God, and like unto the angels, man has evolved from primeval slime as an accidental by-product of the operation of natural selection; that life itself is but a flickering accident in a measureless universe moving without purpose or destiny.

As for good and evil, they are but categories of social convenience, interchangeable over time and space according to the prevailing culture. Saints and fiends, both, are the victims of illusions traceable in the main to glandular defects. Criminals are to be cured by an injection; fanatics by a pill. Morality, heroism, tragedy, alike are anaesthetized before the advance of modern medicine.

This then is what we are to teach our children. And it is depressing enough in all conscience. For man is also a worshipping animal. He craves objects of reverence as he craves objects of beauty and love. Once the great myths lie shattered, and with them the heroes, the saints and the prophets of old, what is there left for men to turn towards but the cold light of science and the unalloyed brainpower of its priesthood – a form of worship but little removed from that of Mammon.

But the loss for men of the myths, above all the loss of the great religious faiths – a loss that is an inescapable by-product of the growth of science and technology – has yet unhappier consequences.

It has too readily been assumed by the so-called humanist that men, once shorn of their belief in a high being, would turn their energies to more worldly things, and their worship of God to love of their fellows. The frantic self-seeking which distinguishes those countries that have benefited most from the advance of science and technology provide some evidence for the first presumption. But the second presumption, that deprived of God men would turn their love towards one another, is not borne out by casual observation. It is not so much the case that feeling is 'drying up' within us. But with so much feeling being chanelled into the aptly-called 'rat-race' – into the pursuit of worldly success and into the pursuit of fashion and prestige pastimes – there is little left to flow directly between people. Yet the thinner runs this flow of feeling between people the more impatient a man becomes to seek satisfactions in the external world of status and glamour, a world buzzing with perpetual expectancy wherein other people play but an incidental role is his schemes of personal triumph.

An age persistently acclaiming its emancipation from imagined Victorian inhibitions about erotic love finds itself curiously uncomfortable in talking about the love of man for his brothers. But the fear of sounding unctuous is itself indicative of the effort required of a generation nurtured, almost exclusively, on material expectations, of opening itself to the experience of affectionate love. Like opening oneself to the experience of God, an act of faith, of bravado even, is involved. For it is only by disclosing one's vulnerability, and affirming the nakedness of one's dependence upon others, can one cross the threshold from isolation into communion.

It is not surprising then that so many today live immured in themselves, watching helplessly as the days and the years slip by without ever touching the warmth of another human being. The reluctance to acknowledge the full extent of one's need of others is, today, reinforced by those fashionable postures of nonchalance and unconcern. It is becoming harder to resist the temptation to play it safe, to 'play it cool', with the result, inevitably, that one lives it cool, cut off from the inner pulse of life. The belief in a personal God, however, helps a man to come closer to others. Not only does it strengthen his hold on psychic realities in a world frantic with ambitions, the same faith that enables him to open his innermost heart to his Maker, enables him also to open it for his fellows.

Only the simple in mind can believe that in the passing away of religious faith humanity has done no more than discarded its primitive superstitions; that a decent community spirit can somehow replace the observances and rituals of religion, and that the moral precepts for a civilized society can as well be founded on the rationality of an enlightened social interest. With the death of God, something in each one of us has died also. In losing a faith that empowered him to surrender to the love and mercy of his Maker, a man lost more than the solace of his faith. He lost that which, by giving impulse to the flow of sympathy and trust within him, led him towards others in the vital experience of love.[1]

---

[1] The common view that cruel wars and persecutions have also been inspired by religious beliefs is too facile to admit as an argument on the other side. Any institution disposing of the immense power and wealth enjoyed over the centuries by the Church could not but tempt ambitious men into political intrigue, corruption and militancy. More important yet, no matter how great the potential beneficence of an idea, it is possible always for men to pervert it to their own interests: every ideology that inspires men can be used also as an instrument of persecution and of conquest by faeatics seeking power. The brave cause of socialism led by Russian revolutionaries issued in an internecine war of indescribably savagery. The cry 'Liberty, Equality, Fraternity', that fired men's hearts also let loose the horrors that drenched the soil of France in blood. The pursuit of 'virtue' gave Robespierre to history. Napoleon's armies of 'liberation' looted and tyrannized over Europe.

So long as men are ambitious for power, any idea that inspires people will be readily exploited in the endeavour to gain the support necessary to wield power. And as with freedom, so with religion one may truly exclaim, 'O Lord, what crimes are committed in thy name!'

II

But disencumbering men of their faith in God is not the only service conferred on mankind by science. In so far as men still cling to a belief in their intrinsic value as human beings, the advance of science provides an opportunity of a yet greater act of emancipation.

Sooner, rather than later, we shall be presented by science with the power to determine the sex of the unborn infant. Within the foreseeable future techniques will be available to determine also its genetical composition. The day is not far off when we shall learn to dispose forever with the need of a mother's womb. Already science is opening up for us a wonderland of computers, automation and cybernetics. Almost anything a man can do a machine can do or soon will be able to do at least as well, and infinitely faster. Scientists are at work on machines that translate, machines that write poetry, machines that compose music, machines that learn to play intellectual games like chess, machines that generate hypotheses. Of course, *man* has made these things: we have not quite reached the stage where machines create other machines of their own volition. Let us take what crumbs of metaphysical comfort we can get. For once we turn from *man*, as a metaphorical embodiment of the extent of human knowledge, to ordinary men and women, we have no choice but to realize that in one attribute after another they are being outdone by contraptions of wire and chemicals. Indeed, science is now successfully exploring substitutes for man's internal organs, a project of mercy to be sure, and with the prospect one day of enabling men to free themselves from subjection to the weakness of human flesh. If machines are becoming like men, men are no less determined to become like machines in a most literal sense.

In the meantime and to a rising chorus of hosannas to the miracles of modern science, the layman – and, beside the sum total of scientific achievement, we are all laymen now – becomes, every day that passes, more of a bewildered spectator to what is happening around him, willy-nilly having to adapt his mode of living to the technology of industry and to the flow of gadgets on to the market. Flattered by the Press for his readership, wooed by the politician for his vote, cajoled by the salesman for his money, how can he escape the feeling that he is naught but a unit of exploitation, one among millions, and as near anonymous as makes no difference?

As he is shunted into the era of automation and freed further from mental and muscular effort, all the syrupy sounds of television, all the baubles and the paraphernalia of soft-living, and all the eupeptic drugs in creation, will not suffice to conceal from him the stark facts of his predicament. He may be taught to play games for his health and to seek recreations that soothe his thwarted instincts. But as an ordinary human being the reins will have slipped from his hands. He will live by the grace of the scientist, destined to become a drone, protected for a time by social institutions and the persisting remnants of a moral tradition, but transparently expendable like some thousand million others heaped like ants over the earth.

Chapter 19

Profit Propelled Growth: 1

Sustained technological advance, I have argued, tends inexorably to destroy the sources of satisfaction of ordinary people regardless of the form of economic or social organization. It is, however, worth distinguishing certain features common to the affluent West, where economic growth is directed in the main by commercial forces, if only because some of these features have become so marked and, to some people, so manifestly vicious that they are apt to obscure, temporarily, the less immediate but ultimately more destructive consequences associated with technological advance *per se*.

Already we have had occasion (in Part IV) to dismiss as untenable the doctrinaire claims made on behalf of the private enterprise system, in particular the claim that it enhances welfare by extending the range of choices open to society. We now turn briefly to some other examples of the more overtly corrupting influences exerted on society by the ceaseless search for profits in a wealthy economy.

(1) The wealthier the economy the greater the opportunities for the so-called growth industries. With an increasing margin of expenditure available for 'luxury items', the chance of making a quick fortune by some new article of wear, or some new mechanical gadget, is in the forefront of the minds of business executives and of hopeful young men as yet unplaced in industry. Indeed, some products that are introduced into the economy as novelties or luxury items – the telephone, the private car, the television set, for example – so influence the growth of the economy as to become necessaries for the mass of the people. The

rapidity and apparent ease with which anyone acting on a lucky hunch can become a millionaire has always been played up in the United States, yet never so persistently as today. One cannot easily escape the welter of success stories about people, young and old, educated and semi-literate, who have become wealthy overnight, so to speak, by gambling on a bright idea or by a series of shrewd transactions, honest, shady, or a mixture of both. As an essential ingredient of the contents of newspapers, popular magazines, and television programmes, such tales have become a part of the daily intake not just of the business community but of society at large. It goes without saying that the overnight fortune is less likely to be made by producing some staple item more efficiently than by inventing some 'gimmick', by discovering some new 'need', or by creating some fashion.

The net gains of the fortune seekers themselves, however, are of less concern to us than the effects on the public at large. The opportunities for quick profits provided by the successful marketing of novelties and gimmicks are further magnified in a wealthy private enterprise system by the formation of a volatile consuming public that has long been severed from the sobering influences of tradition. Indeed, the growth-man's chief hope of maintaining economic momentum in the West lies in the development of just such a consuming public. For, as already observed, the success achieved in producing high levels of expenditure in the affluent society requires the continuous creation of new dis-satisfactions which are made to rise phoenix-like from the ashes of old satisfactions – a process that is facilitated by a consuming public just described, one whose tastes are free of traditional notions of excellence and whose acquisitive impulses are unrestrained by any standards of propriety.

Thus, taste becomes the slave of fashion, and fashion the creature of profits. The ideal consuming public for the wealthy competitive society is one that is 'free-floating' in time, one that can be moulded and segmented and pulled hither and thither by bright-eyed ad men. And if this ideal public has, in fact, so conveniently come into being in economic conditions of near-surfeit[1] some thanks are due also to the

---

[1] I have no doubt that redistributive policies would raise aggregate expenditure even in the absence of sales promotion. But it is conventional to accept as a political datum the existing structure of disposable income. With the given structure of distribution of disposable purchasing power, the US is a near surfeit economy in the sense that sales pressure and created obsolescence are necessary to maintain the propensity to spend.

pronouncements of the technocrats who bid us seek emancipation by embracing the novel idea that perpetual and accelerating change is the essence of the new civilization, a civilization in which social norms have no time to form and in which concepts of right and wrong are functional and ephemeral.

II

(2) Owing to high employment and post-war affluence, one of the fastest growing markets in the West, just now, is that drawing its substance from the pockets of juveniles. Not surprisingly, the US provides an outstanding example, with the luxury expenditure of American 'teenagers' (between thirteen and seventeen years old) averaging (in 1965) some seven hundred dollars a year. Given spare cash on this scale, one need only bear in mind the impetuousness and gullibility of youth, now exposed daily to the suggestions of teenaged magazines and to high-powered advertising media, to appreciate the boundless confidences with which so many businessmen view their future prospects. Using the magic pipe provided by Madison Avenue, private enterprise has taken on a new role as Pied Piper of Hamelin followed by hordes of youngsters jingling their money and tumbling over themselves to be 'with it', without of course the faintest notion of what they are 'with' or where they are going. And it seems scarcely credible that eminent economists on both sides of the Atlantic continue with all solemnity to apply themselves to the study of means whereby national outputs can be expanded more rapidly at a time when so large a portion of any additional output caters to this display of puerile extravagance and frantic go-go.

This new manifestation of commercial growth is not merely outlandish, its repercussions on society are pernicious. For though assertive impulses associated with the process of growing up can admittedly bring about occasional tension between old and young even in stable societies, the differences in outlook between a youth and his father are considerably aggravated by this gathering pace of change. Up to a generation ago it was common enough for a young man to forsake his father's gods at some stage in his life, yet he generally managed to do so without estranging himself completely from his elders. Differences of opinion between generations was not incompatible with sympathetic communication between them. If the young rebel forsook his father's gods he generally embraced new ones, and his defiance was tempered by the outward forms of respect for parents so that differences in opinions notwithstanding, they could still partake in the common fund of affection that unites a family. Today, with the dissolution of a common frame of ethical reference, communication between the generations appears to be breaking down. Contempt rather than defiance has come to mark the attitude of the young towards their elders. After all, what is there to defy, apart from the police, when conventional morality has all but withered away? In a commercialized society in which the most money is made by fanning the flames of minor vices – envy, lust, vanity, avarice – a society in which status and success are the overt rewards of sustained self-seeking, it is no great wonder that utter cynicism is in vogue with the young. In so far as this cynicism breeds among the young a negative couldn't-care-less attitude towards adult approval, they are the more readily exploitable by the commercial purveyors of frippery and feathers.

And never was a younger generation so ill-equipped to withstand the siren songs of the entrepreneurs. Nor poverty, nor filial bonds, nor church authority, nor tradition, nor idealism, nor inhibition of any sort stand between them and the realization of any freak of fancy that enters their TV-heated imaginations. Social workers and journalists who have entered the candy-and-tinsel world that teenagers increasingly seek to inhabit, and have witnessed their mawkish raptures, their cultivated gluttony, their drug sessions, and their stylized seductions, are uncertain whether to be appalled or exhilarated by these near-hysterical attempts of the young to divest themselves of responsibility. But the comforting 'frank and free' epithets, with which the imperturbable progressive is wont to dismiss it all, just do not stick. This 'permissive' world that is emerging is not a product of any new Enlightenment; no principle or ethic is involved; no idealism pervades it. Its genesis is the moral vacuum created by the bewilderment of parents caught in a dissolving society. The adjective, moreover, belies its nature. Inasmuch as it imposes on the young the strain of repressing their individuality in the engrossing task of conforming to all the rages of juvenile fashion, it is all but compulsive.[1] For many of these young people only the exacting demands of a competitive and technically sophisticated civilization stand between them and their surrender to the amoral arcadia of the new permissiveness.

[1] Among all too many of the young, sexual experience too has become not merely permissive. It has become mandatory. Nor is it enough simply to make love. Like justice, it must not only be done; it must be seen to be done.

In such a milieu, no one need wonder that crime, robbery with violence in particular, is one of our fast-growing industries. To the uncluttered conscience of the young, mundane considerations preponderate. These include the fact that the crime industry is increasing in efficiency: the rewards are larger and the chances of being caught are smaller than they used to be; and the fact also that the public is seemingly more prone to sympathize with the criminal rather than with the police.

And if the deterrents are weaker, the incentives are stronger. The visions portrayed by the glossy magazines of a perpetual *dolce vita* to be enjoyed by a young, smart, ruthlessly selfish, fast-moving, freely-spending clique act as a standing temptation to the impressionable young today to make good the deficiencies of talent or fortune by crime rather than by industry.

III

(3) In a centrally-controlled economy such as that of the U S S R, the rapid spread of higher education in the post-war period has provided people with both a rising standard of consumption, and a dependable and potent source of anxiety. But in the predominantly commercially-directed economy, in the U S more than the U K, the growth of anxiety among students and parents has become near pathological. Since the entrance to the universities is regarded, not without reason, as the indispensable first step on the ladder to worldly success, and subsequent degrees as effective passports into the élite occupations of high status and earnings, open cheating during school examinations has become endemic.[1] The response of commerce, with the connivance if not the active support of high schools and colleges, to the fears that afflict a growing number of students could have been predicted: an endless stream of hastily contrived textbooks (most of them directed towards some specific course), of collections of lecture notes (sometimes mimeographed on the campus), of concentrated cram courses in pamphlet form, of paperbacks congested with potted knowledge, and of digests of exam questions complete with model answers.

[1] According to a report in *Newsweek* (21st March, 1966): 'Columbia University's Dr Allen Barton who supervised a study of ninety-nine colleges, a study which concluded half the students in the sample had cheated, believes high school cheating is even more prevalent. . . .'

And why not? American universities are moving with the tide and are on the way to transforming themselves into vast automated degree-punching factories, equipped with computers, closed-circuit television, and rows of teaching machines. At one end of the factory the raw freshmen are sucked in and, with the minimum of human contact, are passed from process to process, imbibing information on the way, regurgitating it at set intervals to be inspected by machines. If not revealed defective they will emerge at the other end, exhausted perhaps, but ready to be stamped with the firm's warranty. Admittedly, much graduate teaching is still in the handloom stage, and the finished product of high technical excellence. None the less, with the inevitable devaluation of the bachelor's degree, and the consequent growth in the population of post-graduate aspirants, one may confidently anticipate some extension of the principles of mass-production to the training courses for higher degrees.

I do not argue that this application of technology to teaching methods is less efficient. If students could dehumanize themselves as readily as these universities, they could well become more knowledgeable than those students trained by more traditional methods. But if they cannot; if they resist the new technology, what then? Not surprisingly there is a growing revolt against the Orwellian features of the new automated education. It is not altogether fantastic for a student to feel he is being machine-cut, pressed, moulded and trimmed to fit into a complex industrial system that is geared to churn out endless streams of plastic and gadgetry for a mass consumption society; one, apparently, that has no interest in his latent idealism nor cares for his resentments or anxieties – save as they reduce his productivity.

Thinking along such lines one cannot help feeling that one of the chief explanations of student demonstrations and student protests is not to be sought in the immediate issues or events connected with them, but in the less articulate repudiation by many students of the emergent features of our incipient mega-universities, and of the sort of society which they represent. The anti-social behaviour of beatniks, hippies, provos and other untidy-looking groups, are more obviously – perhaps too obviously – interpretable as an obstinate protest against the anonymity, the aimlessness, the anomie of the technological society; one in which the gradual acceptance of efficiency as a universal norm must prove fatal to the traditional humanitarian values.

The problems of the staffing of these new metropolitan-type universities appear to be met by adopting methods familiar to such competitive industries as film-making or big league football. Academic stars, too, have become increasingly mobile, tending to move to where the contracts are fattest, or at least, to those institutes where the tangible advantages are greatest. A substantial part of the duties of the senior staff members of American universities consists of organizing appeals for the funds necessary to continue their bidding and counter-bidding for the services of academic VIPs.

The effects of this competitive scramble on standards of scholarship and of teaching remain to be seen. One may, however, ascribe to it the growing impatience to have published work to one's credit. And the knowledge that others also are striving to break into print adds further to the pressure to submit one's work the sooner, before it is anticipated by others. The effect of this pressure to 'get in' first, at a time when rapidly increasing technical and specialized knowledge has augmented the difficulties of editing a scientific journal, goes some way to explain the extent of 'premature publication' in journals – the number of papers that are inelegant, unfinished or unintelligible. To this competitive system one may also ascribe a marked preference by competent staff members for research as against teaching, a preference that the university has to respect if it is to be able to attract to its faculties the big names and the promising young men.

These developments, an extension of the market-place, with its truck-and-barter manoeuvres, to the big business of higher education, are a far cry from the traditional conception of the universities as seats of learning. Far also is the current conception of education from that which for centuries inspired reformers and philosophers, that of education as a good in itself, involving, as it should, a prolonged period of study, discourse and reflection, designed in the main to foster the spirit of inquiry, to enlarge the understanding, and to refine the sensibilities. Above all, education was looked to as an influence for bringing people closer through a common appreciation of history, of the natural world, and of their heritage of art and literature.

In today's world, prostrate before the notion of economic growth, the idea of education as an end in itself has a distinctly nostalgic flavour. Adult education is increasingly thought of as a means to material ends – even where the ends tie in with democratic goals such as that of equalizing the structure of earnings. The greater part of university education today is unadulterated vocational training, the degree associated with it aptly dubbed the meal ticket.

It may be protested that this feverish post-war expansion of vocational education at least brings us closer to the ideal of universal equality of opportunity. Yet, according as we realize this ideal the closer we approach a fully-working meritocracy; a system of society in which rewards are based ultimately on the manifest inequalities of intellectual and artistic endowment – in effect, then, on pure accident of birth. The culmination of these trends will issue perhaps in a yet more efficient society but hardly a more just society, and possibly one that is a great deal more irksome, indeed mortifying, to the lower echelons than was, say, the eighteenth century system of landed aristocracy in Britain.

Chapter 20

Profit Propelled Growth: 2

I

(4) Although the thwarted instincts of men living in an anonymous and unintegrated civilization have made them vulnerable to protest movements impatient to explore the world of the senses, in their narrow meaning, the steam behind the movement for the abolition of all forms of censorship, and more specifically in favour of unrestricted freedom in the presentation of all erotic and related matter, is predominantly commercial. With the new mass media and the growing potential of mass markets there develops an insatiable public demand for entertainment. In response there appears a perpetual search among the army of writers, artists and producers, for that which is a little different; for that which will catch the public's fancy. But the search for novelty is the enemy of the excellent. So, more obviously, is the search for commercial success. Even among the nucleus of talent in the army of those catering to mass entertainment there is little material incentive to subject themselves to the exacting discipline of sustained artistic endeavour. Far simpler, and far more commercially rewarding, it is to compel attention by shock tactics, especially those involved in flouting the remnants of convention and tabu. Sex lends itself admirably for this purpose. Already 'men's magazines', *avant-garde* literature, experimental cinema, and the good fight of Anglo-Saxon writers for the freedom to use four-letter words, have accustomed the public to ingest increasing doses of bowdlerized pornography.

However, the lack of sustained protest is indicative not only of tolerance but also of the bewilderment of an age that is witnessing the collapse of all norms of taste and propriety. It is also indicative of public timidity before journalistic sophistry about the value of erotic art forms. Indeed, to be in tune with the times, one is expected to respond with an outward show of coolness, suppressing excitements or oral-aggressive feelings, aroused by highly salacious art forms: suppressing also any feelings of anxiety. For to confess misgivings about the value of being exposed to increasing doses of pornography is to open oneself to charges of illiberalism, if not also of obscenity. As things stand then, the question is not so much whether but when will the public succumb to the pressure of interested groups – well-meaning liberals as well as congenital voyeurs, pulp writers, enterprising publishers and impresarios – for the removal of all legal censorship and restraint.

The arguments for extending licence are not new. Indeed, they are more of historic than of current interest. The popular liberal arguments turn on thin-edge-of-the-wedge themes and on the social or aesthetic consequences of subjecting artistic and literary inspiration to the veto of the authorities. The good liberal will readily admit the possibility of abuses but, he insists, an open society must run such risks in order that artistic expression may flourish and enrich the imaginative experience and thus the lives of its citizens. To the argument that literature is invariably impoverished by any restraint, legal or social, that prohibits the treatment of any aspect of life – a proposition that compels us to ponder on the unrealized potential of a Dickens, a Hardy or a Conrad – we may add the hedonistic view that pure pornography be recognized as an art form that affords pleasure and excitement to some people, and also the therapeutic view (currently, however, in ill odour among psychiatrists) that depiction of sexual extravagances, perversions and cruelties, either in literature or on the stage or screen, tends to air our repressed fantasies, purge us of our tensions, and so improve our emotional health.

These arguments for an extension of licence are somewhat removed from the realities of the interests involved. None the less, those who accept them ought to recognize the difficulties they lead to. Inasmuch as one or other of such arguments is believed to justify the removal of any particular kind of censorship it justifies also the removal of *all* kinds of censorship. If, in the defence of freedom of expression, it is affirmed that anything done by men or women, or anything thought by men or women, is a part of life, and, *therefore*, a potential art form, we have excluded nothing. If James Joyce is permitted to follow his hero into the toilet so as to reveal certain aspects of his character, what obscene or brutal incidents cannot be absolved on the grounds of character revelation? If any controversial book or play is to be vindicated by its capacity to stir thought or feeling in a man, then again there can be no objection to sexual intimacies performed on the stage if the drama 'calls for it'. Neither can there be any objection to any stage presentation of homosexual, incestuous or other perverse sexual practices, performed in all circumstance and detail. For such a performance would undoubtedly reveal something of the character of the participants and could be counted upon to excite some feelings among the spectators. And what of performances of physical sadism, the exquisite torture of naked bodies, the crucifixion of squealing infants, or any other such inspired scene designed to pluck sharply at the raw ends of our nerves? After all, the resultant excitement, the shock or horror, or savage relish, are all deeply-felt experiences – though we must allow for the possibility over time of our appetites becoming jaded for lack of yet stronger fare.

Whatever the answer, the fact remains that until recently private interests were condemned to scavenging odd nuggets of alloyed pornography found lying about the banned entrance to a mine of apparently unlimited commercial potential. It may be a brave gesture to open up the entrance, another challenge maybe. But the result of the experiment, even if not disastrous, is hardly likely to promote the happiness of mankind.

It is idle to pretend that after passing through a dark period of confused counsels, a more mature society is now attempting no more than to restore to health and freedom natural instincts erroneously repressed. Recourse to such words as 'frank', 'open', 'God-given', and to such phrases as 'the naked beauty of woman's body having inspired the greatest artists over the centuries', in justification of entertainment that depends for its drawing power on the hints of scenes of sizzling salacity is characteristic of the hypocrisy and irresponsibility of the age. *Hypocrisy* because, though there will always be borderline cases, there are distinctions between art that enables the human form and between erotic art and pornographic art. And to cloak a manifest appeal to voyeurism with phrases about the body beautiful, or unflinching realism, is as unsubtle as it is unsavoury. Erotic picture magazines displaying the white against black starkness of massive thighs, of swollen breasts and buttocks in suggestive poses offer something beyond simple aesthetic pleasure to their beholders. Highly-spiced sadistic fiction has consequences other than providing its readers with visceral enjoyment. *Irresponsibility*, because such words serve to ignore the possibility that this exciting movement to establish, surreptitiously or otherwise, pornography as an everyday feature of social life has far-reaching consequences which, in our impetuous search for more goodies of whatever nature or shape, we have so far neglected to think about. Before allowing ourselves to be whirled along into the all-permissive society we might have the humility to engage in a little soul-searching.

For one thing, we no longer live in a stable society, much less a mature one, but a society being rent apart by the torrential forces of modern technology and modern communications. In fact, a society in a state of rapid dissolution. This is not the time to be searching for lost innocence. It is not as if we are, or ever could be made like, the primitive Tahitian islanders discovered by Captain Cook, who openly enjoyed their sexual activities and found every prospect pleasing. And if we could be, the medium of transfiguration is not likely to have much affinity with those employed by commercial interests that have done so much to foster among the young a view of modern science as an irresistible Santa harnessed to the task of providing humanity with the technical paraphernalia necessary to a life of unlimited self-indulgence. For many of them, 'the pill' is regarded as a symbol of emancipation from penalties once exacted by nature and society. For them, guilt 'is out'. They are 'not interested in suffering'. As though it will be possible to grow without being weaned; as though gratification can be known without yearning; as though life can be experienced without suffering; as though music can be composed on a single note. Neither is it true that guilt is but a superfluous adjunct of man's personality, a negative force only, a consequence of too repressive a childhood. It is more than conceivable that a sense of original sin, though nourished by myth, is rooted in man's psyche, and that his sustained attempts at reparation, his endless search for grace, is a source of creative effort in art, music, literature.

At all events, the growing market for pornographic literature and for quasi-pornographic entertainment is one of the clearest symptoms of widespread maladjustment. For complex reasons associated with the pace and pressure of modern life, all too many adults who find themselves unable to attain normal sexual fulfilment are tempted by the new super-carnal art to withdraw further from the potential reality of human experience, set by biological limitations, into the gaping jaws of fantasy – so isolating themselves further from affectionate communication with others. Indeed, this is inevitable. Pornographic-fed fantasies tend to intensify sexual fetishism – the primitive fantasied separation and auto-animation of body parts – a fetishism that is, incidentally, encouraged by fashions directed to a concealing-revealing cut of outer and under garments. According as sexual excitement becomes habitually directed towards, and becomes, dependent upon such sexual fetishism, so must the victim excite himself with fantasies that are by nature unfulfillable. In torment he may turn to perverse or even criminal practices. Since it is the nature of such fantasies that they cannot be consummated in the real world, all measures that tend towards their systematic encouragement increase the risk of ultimate sexual frustration and despair.

II

The movement to legalize pornography is one with the movement to legalize the sale of drugs – and for motives that have little in common with John Stuart Mill's eloquent plea for liberty. In a civilization, where sexual frustrations are magnified by a rising tide of commercially inspired and quite unrealizable expectations, such movements gather their force from a desperate search for some magic potion to spark off buried instincts, or some catalyst to cleave open the kernels of sensation.

Alcoholics who cannot resist a drink would be wise to vote for the closing of public bars. In a civilization as vulnerable as ours is to the many corrupting influences of commercial enterprise, we should have the prudence to resist the invitation to 'crash through the sex barrier'.[1]

---

[1] A time when the study by Johnson and Masters, *Human Sexual Response* (May 1966), is arousing interest among the critics provides an opportunity of expressing doubts also about this approach to the mid-century obsession with sex. If there were no other choice, the recent and engagingly pathetic 'refreshingly frank discussion' phase is to be preferred to the yet more futile phase that would disseminate among the general public the findings of prolonged and detached studies of the physiology of sex. Though it is generally conceded that there may be more in the human sex relation than can be satisfactorily explained in physical terms, and that there are nuances of pleasure and intimacy incompletely revealed by indices of performance and measure of orgasm, the ingenuous liberal will persist in his quest for truth. Why not measure all that can be measured today, and tomorrow we shall measure more? Why not let the light of day into dark places, and so combat error and superstition? Why not, indeed, in this heroic age of barrier-crashing? Yet one does wonder just what extra dimension people hope to discover on emerging. After all, their manifest impatience to break through each new 'barrier' itself arises from the growing frustrations of a way of life that is a by-product of so many other much-heralded break-throughs.

Already we have touched on some of the consequences on our lives of being deprived of the warmth of myth and mystery by the advance of knowledge. In

The last word must be with Plato, a man who was more fearful of corruption through freedom than through tyranny. The good life is the whole life, a harmony, each attribute being present in just proportion. Each part of a man's nature can be likened to a musical instrument that has its place in the full orchestra. If all play in harmony the ensuing sound is rich and musical. If some instruments are played too loudly and others are neglected the resulting sound is harsh, discordant, perhaps unbearable.

The rapid economic growth of the West over the last half century and especially the last two decades, has not yet been accomplished without traumatic effects on their populations. Tension is everywhere more evident than harmony, disproportion more evident than porportion. The gross overdevelopment of the acquisitive instinct has its genesis in the industrial free enterprise system of the Classical economists. The increasing obsession with sex, and with sexual display masquerading as fashion; the technique of distilling the carnality of sex, as though it were an essence to be poured lavishly into all forms of modern entertainment, these too owe much to private enterprise and advertising. The result, today, with commerce eagerly reacting to the expectations of excitement it has done so much to create, is the gross displacement of a social libido. And there are no countervailing forces at work today to coax it back into a proper scheme of things. Since there is no road back there is, alas, the undeniable inclination to move 'forward'. Indeed, with the Church in disarray, with the 'experts' divided and the public perplexed, it is not to be expected that the law will hold out much longer against the mounting commercial pressure, backed by naïve writers and liberals, to abolish all forms of censorship leaving a morally fragile and edgy society to cope with the flood as best it can.

---

so far as knowledge supplants spontaneity it also reduces the intensity of a man's experience. Detailed contemplation of the particular ways in which our reflexes function is more apt to hinder than to help them. If we think too closely about the process of absorbing information from, say, the act of reading a book, we will find it harder to continue the process. By trying to watch ourselves thinking, the thinking itself falters to a halt. An inescapable consciousness of the phases and chemistry of the sexual act must serve also to weaken its spontaneity and to qualify that surrender to the upsurge of feeling necessary for its fulfilment.

Chapter 21

The Cult of Efficiency

I

We have already indicated in an earlier chapter that the concept of expanding choices has little application to the range of opportunities that face working men. The loss of aesthetic and instinctual gratification suffered by ordinary working men over two centuries of technological innovation that changed them from artisans and craftsmen into machine-minders and dial-readers must remain a matter of speculation. It need not, however, be supposed that every phase of this historical transformation produced a change for the worse: it may well be that, beginning from some period in the first half of the nineteenth century, the conditions of work have been steadily improving. Yet the conditions of work, including the social facilities provided, may not be the chief factors contributing to the satisfaction derived by men from their daily tasks. It is more than just possible that the chief source of men's satisfaction resides in the kind of work they are called upon to perform and on the regard in which the product of their work is held by their fellows. Two centuries ago, before the 'industrial revolution' was properly launched, a skilled workman in this country was a craftsman. Whether he worked in wood, clay, leather, stone, metal or glass, he was the master of his material, and the thing he produced grew in his hands from the substance of the earth to the finished article. He was ever-mindful that he was a member of an honoured craft; that he had reached his position after a long apprenticeship; and he took legitimate pride in the excellence of his work.

We are far removed today from that state of society in which craftsmen worked with their own tools in transforming the material into the

148

finished product. And though few workmen alive will have known a situation when it was otherwise, it does not follow that no loss is experienced. Certainly those who have lived through the transitional phases have borne eloquent testimony to their misgivings. Leaving aside such episodes of open resistance to technological improvements, there is no lack of expressions of sadness and regret in the English literature at the passing of the skilled hand-worker. One that comes to mind is the touching lament reproduced from George Sturt's *The Wheelwright's Shop*: 'Of course wages are higher – many a workman today receives a larger income than I was ever able to get as "profit" when I was an employer. But no higher wage, no income, will buy for men that satisfaction which of old – until machinery made drudges of them – streamed into their muscles all day long from close contact with iron, timber, clay, wind and wave, horse-strength. It tingled up in the niceties of touch, sight, scent. The very ears unawares received it, as when the plane went ringing over the wood, or the exact chisel went tapping in (under the mallet) to the hard ash with gentle sound. But these intimacies are over. Although they have so much more leisure men can now take little solace in life, of the sort the skilled handwork used to yield them. Just as the seaman today has to face the stokehole rather than the gale, and knows more of heatwaves than of seawaves, so throughout. In what was once the wheelwright's shop, where Englishmen grew friendly with the grain of timber and with sharp tools, nowadays untrained youths wait upon machines, hardly knowing oak from ash or caring for the qualities of either.'

The growing popularity of do-it-yourself kits and craft hobbies is evidence surely of a search to recapture something of the deep satisfaction enjoyed by the craftsmen of old that comes of mastering the material and creating with the hands. The pity of it is that such hobbies can be enjoyed only briefly after the day's work, or at week-ends, instead of being the daily work itself. Of course, we are assured by the technocrats that once we reach the promised land of Newfanglia the opportunities for leisurely enjoyments – at least in the 'long run' after all the initial economic disturbances have been overcome – will be immense. To the engineering cast of mind, work, any kind of work, is input only; it is the effort expended in producing output. Since *all* input is regarded as a 'disutility', and *all* output as a 'utility', efficiency consists of reducing the ratio of input to output. If the engineer continues thus to lighten the burden of man's toil, the day must dawn when the curse of Adam is thrown off, and man forever freed from the daily grind. He need thereafter do only the sort of work that interests him, and then only when he feels the inclination. Surely a dazzling prospect for man!

But what of the innate needs of ordinary men? It is not just a question of the limits to leisure that can be enjoyed: few of the rich, in fact, devote themselves full time to the hectic pursuit of pleasure. Many of them adopt causes, or continue to engage in empire-building of sorts: for most men need to feel that their work matters to society – a need that is harder to fulfil as society becomes increasingly more impersonal. The creative satisfaction enjoyed by the craftsman of old, critical though it was in the pattern of his well-being, did not of itself suffice. Social recognition of his work must be added thereto before his contentment was assured. If a master-baker, displaced by the invention of completely automatic ovens, were so fortunate as to be compensated with a sum of money enabling him to buy a set of his old-fashioned ovens and withal to live comfortably, though he could now continue to bake his five hundred loaves a day, he would be unlikely to continue it as a hobby. What he creates as a hobby may well be an excellent thing, or it may not be. His friends may admire it or they may just be polite about it. But whatever their response, it is plain enough that it does not matter very much to others whether he continues or discontinues with the work. And this is a fact that makes all the difference to the basic self-respect of our displaced baker. Even a great artist will not escape a feeling of bitterness if society pays no heed to his work. And the ordinary worker stands in need of more reassurance than the great artist. For the craftsman who produces directly for a community that both appreciates and needs the product of his hand and brain, and evinces that need by a readiness to pay for his skill, there is that blessed feeling of belonging and of being an indispensable part of the daily life of his community. Whatever else may have been lacking in that smaller scale of society in which the yeoman tilled the soil and masters and apprentices worked with patient skill at their craft, there was always this unassailable self-respect and, therefore, that abiding sense of security which is no common thing in the feverish jostling world of today.

And not only a sense of our own worth but a sense of the worth of others is being lost in pursuit of efficiency. The more we become fascinated with the measurable aspects of human achievement the easier it is to slip into a frame of mind that judges people according to numerical systems and that ranks their worth on some scale of efficiency. In time we lose sight both of the subtle and engaging facets of the character of each individual and of the intrinsic value of each human life. In continually directing our calculations to the uses of other men, regarded as means to the attainment of material ends, the modern world's preoccupation with efficiency tends to blunt our moral sensibilities.[1]

II

There are other sources of human gratification, equally unmeasurable by the engineer's yardstick, that are lost sight of in the obsessive scramble of the rich countries to exploit every technological opportunity. Some of the features incidental to the mode of production and which technocrats, in their overriding concern with efficiency, would regard as irrelevant turn out on inspection to contribute far more to the welfare of the worker than the direct worth of the output so produced. An open, easy and full-hearted relationship with one's fellows, for instance, is not something that can be bought on the market or willed into being. The indispensable ingredient of such a relationship is mutual trust, a quality nurtured in the small agrarian society based on mutual dependence, but one of the first casualties when such a society is uprooted from the soil and sucked into the vortex of modern capitalism.

It is undeniably more efficient that a child should imbibe his amusement from the television screen rather than his parents' time and energy be diverted to the telling of bedtime stories. More efficient, also, to turn the knob of a panel in order to capture the music of a celebrated symphony orchestra than to arrange, instead, a solo or duet performance by members of the family. On an aesthetic plane, the reproduction

[1] How else does one explain the lack of organized protest at the manifestly immoral basis of the draft selection procedures of the United States Government (Spring 1966). Incredible though it seems the examination system was designed to separate the efficient members of the community from the less efficient, those in the latter category being conscripted into the armed forces as being, in effect, more expendable to their country. It is a further reflection of the moral obtuseness of our times that a large part of the outcry against these methods of selection, by student groups and other organizations, was directed towards the inefficiency and 'unfairness' of the tests employed – there being allegations that the exam questions favoured the science student as against the art student, the educated against the uneducated, and, therefore, the rich against the poor and the white against the coloured. Employ some 'ideal' test in a thoroughgoing meritocracy and, apparently, such protests would vanish.

on a modern record-player of the voice of some great singer is certain
to be superior to the sound produced by a man's daughter playing the
piano, or the harpsichord. Yet with the passing of these once-common
domestic occasions, victims of technological progress, some essential
sweetness in the lives of men has also passed away. And it must be said
again, that although these options are not necessarily closed to us merely
because we now have, in addition, gramophones, radios and television
sets, their reality is effectively destroyed. Just as in the passing of the
independent craftsman, what matters is the altered social significance
of these activities in the modern world. The old-time family evening,
entertaining each other with song, music or reading, is a pretty thing
yet, and in defying the high-powered entertainment world of today,
brave even to poignancy. But when the sound of music can flood a
room at a flick of a finger, nobody depends any longer for his comfort
or cheer upon the affection of his family, the alacrity of his neighbours,
or the heartiness of the assembled company. It must be owned that
efficiency has triumphed, and the pleasure that once flowed between
player and listener in the home, and the singing in which the family
would join and warm to each other – these things, in the West, belong
to the world we have lost.

III

Passing on to the teaching machines that are currently being developed,
it is readily granted that the high hopes placed on them by our most
spirited pace-setters will be fulfilled, and that their gradual improvement
will enable future generations to be taught more efficiently than students
are taught today. As for the university-of-the-air project mooted by our
go-ahead politicians, it is all too plausible a vision of the morrow. As
surely as efficiency remains the touchstone, it will be realized in the not-
too-distant-future. After all, it does not require a particularly bright
technocrat to pose the question: why pay several score lecturers to teach
the same subject in different universities in Britain when the growing
army of undergraduates, hungry for the 'meal-ticket' and increasingly
fearful of not getting the very best, could all simultaneously tune in to
some silver-tongued super-lecturer? Televised lectures would be supplemented by auto-instructional programmes in the homes as an efficient
and highly economical substitute for conventional tutorials and
seminars. Indeed, in view of the existing technological possibilities, it is

legitimate to doubt whether the universities as we know them today, as seats both of teaching and learning, will survive the turn of the century.

Yet if people are to be taught more effectively in the future while employing but a fraction of the teaching resources required today, there will also be a loss, the unmeasurable loss of human contact. Just as television has already succeeded in fragmenting the family, and in impoverishing the common fund of mutual experience through which the sense of family is nourished, so also must television apparatus and the teaching machines that are being installed in our universities and our schools, serve in time to isolate people further. The youngster of today, seen from the future, is a victim of the wastes of conventional teaching methods and is, consequently, less proficient than the youngster of tomorrow. But today, at least, he is held together in companionship with his classmates – together with them to exult and despair, to groan and to laugh – sharing with them the vital interchanges of sympathy that accompanies their learning through a teacher with, and through whom, whether they mostly love him or hate him, they explore the resources of human feeling.

With this crucial factor in mind one may appreciate the acknowledged difficulty of giving impetus in the newly built suburbs and towns to something resembling a community spirit – something that was common enough in yesterday's slums which, for all the dirt and distress, had in them much that was warmly human. Indeed the new neighbourhoods are apt to degenerate into 'dormitory areas' in which people of like circumstances occupy the houses, or blocks of flats, within a precinct. Each family, nay, each member of each family, has or soon hopes to have his own television set and private car, the elegant instruments of his estrangement from others. Is it even conceivable for a community to take root in a neighbourhood teeming with cars, transistors, and television sets, in which people have no need and no care to know the names of their itinerant neighbours?

We are realizing, belatedly, that a sense of community is not a synthetic product to be created by a skilful agency employing a variety of appeals. The sense of community requires, above all, the fact of community; an environment of direct human interdependence. And though scientists and scholars may still be able to share intellectual experiences at some point along the extending frontiers of knowledge, for the common man this prospect does not exist. For him, the doors of communication with his fellows, indeed with his family, are gradually

closing as his overt need of them disappears before the relentless advance
of an all-embracing technology.

In the older forms of social organization which began to disappear in
the early nineteenth century it was just this inescapable fact of close
interdependence that held the family and the community together. In
the historical circumstances the interdependence was inevitable, yet
there was unabashed satisfaction in affirming it. The centripetal forces
of modern transport and communications had yet to emerge. In the
meantime, in village or town, the lives of the inhabitants were dominated
by local events. Narrow though their lives might appear by our megalo-
politan standards they had, rich and poor, young and old, their place in
the natural order of things, a settled relationship to one another guided
by a network of custom and mutual obligation. Inevitably, then they
were, all of them, at the centre of the gossip and the interest, all of them
part of the prior and absorbing concern of the community they dwelt in.

IV

Generations have passed, and, like the woods and hedges that sheltered
it, the rich local life centred on township, parish and village, has been
uprooted and blown away by the winds of change. Today no refuge
remains from the desperate universal clamour for more efficiency, more
excitement, and more novelty that goads us furiously onward, competing, accumulating, innovating – and inevitably destroying. Every step
forward in technological progress, and particularly in the things most
eagerly anticipated – swifter travel, depersonalized services, all the push-
button comforts and round-the-clock synthetic entertainment that are
promised us – effectively transfers our dependence upon other human
beings to dependence upon machines[1] and, therefore, unavoidably con-

---

[1]The era is dawning in which film, television and programmed material will
substitute for human teachers; in which the duties of hospital nurses will be
taken over by patient-monitoring devices, and medical diagnoses performed
by computers. While office staff and skilled workers are being automated into
obsolescence, and executives replaced by decision-making machines, game-
playing machines are rendering human partners unnecessary. As for sex, for
procreative purposes, it is already something of an anachronism. Advances in
genetics are about to make fathers expendable; and with the perfection of the
mechanical womb, mothers also will become superfluous. We cannot be far
from the day of the conversation-machine that will relieve us of obligation to
greet politely the occasional recognizable human that strays across our path.

stricts yet further the direct flow of understanding and sympathy between people. Thus in the unending pursuit of progress men are driven even farther apart and come to depend instead, for all their services and experiences, directly upon the creations of technology.

Part VI

Conclusion and Appendices

Chapter 22

Concluding Remarks

I

At the close of our journey it will be useful for the reader to look back over the terrain we have covered and, with the help of some further remarks, to pick out the main features.

This volume begins by suggesting that the preoccupation with 'index economics' – the state of our foreign reserves, interest rate changes, export performance, price movements and other economic events bearing on the 'health' of the economy – leaves us little time to think anew about the social rationale of today's highly developed economies and the goals they should set themselves. Thus, men in authority, immersed in the day-to-day problems of the economy, fail to re-examine, in the light of new circumstances, the validity of the economic presumptions in favour of such traditional long-term goals as competition, free trade, expanding markets and faster economic growth.

There is, of course, some excuse for this persisting concern with what may be called the small change of economics rather than with fundamental issues, at least in the post-war period. For it has been apparently one of recurring economic crises – or, rather, pseudo crises, since apart from an alleged propensity to import too much[1] there is little that is seriously at fault in the British economy. If there were a tendency over

[1]Though only if we include in imports current military expenditure and current long-term lending abroad. Indeed, if we ignore the problem of the sterling balances, our balance of payments over the last six years appears to be stronger than that of any of the Common Market countries. Some of the evidence for this belief may be found in an excellent paper by W. A. P. Manser, 'The UK Balance of payments – A Bar to the European Community?' (*Westminster Bank Review*, November 1966).

recent years for imports to outrun exports, it could in any case have been easier to correct had we been less eager to lend abroad, less determined to play a role as international policeman, and more willing, on occasion, to impose quantitive controls on any of a wide range of relatively expendable imports. Be that as it may, since the additional exports required to balance our excess of imports would take up hardly more than one per cent of our national product – less than the amount by which, on the average, our national product increases each year – it is manifest nonsense to talk about the drastic efforts we must make in order to 'pay our way in the world'.

As for the post-war inflation, in Britain, at least, it is attributable in part to rising material expectations explicitly encouraged by successive governments. More important perhaps, implicit political constraints, in particular the existing commitment to an inflationary level of employment and a pegged exchange rate, have caused minor crises and then exaggerated their seriousness. Thus, there is a marked reluctance in financial and government circles to face the possibility that price stability may be inconsistent with a 98 per cent level of employment, at least in the absence of near-total controls. There is no less of a reluctance to envisage the possibility of establishing a flexible exchange rate for sterling. As a result whenever our imports tend to exceed our exports, and holders of sterling become jittery, we can react only in one way: raise Bank Rate and exert a downward pressure on the whole economy, a tortuous and unnecessary process. Frequent and harsh ministerial warnings, intended to make the headlines, have the further effect of magnifying the difficulty out of all economic proportion and of conveying the impression to the public, at home and abroad, of a nation tottering towards insolvency.

Notwithstanding our lack of finesse in economic matters we shall, given enough time, succeed in balancing our foreign transactions and may even generate an export surplus before, again, returning to a situation of import surplus. This, however, is not the issue. What is the issue are the sort of measures needed to promote a more stable and less crisis-prone economic climate. If we are willing to divest ourselves of much unnecessary expertise and to turn from the fascination of balance-of-payments movements to matters of greater economic moment, we should be thinking hard about ways of introducing a much higher degree of flexibility into the exchange rate and the money supply. To the extent we succeed we shall be able to leave the balance of payments to look after itself and also, therefore, to formulate domestic policies by reference to purely domestic needs: not, as at present by reference to the gold reserves, to the fears or hopes of speculators, or to the mood of Zurich bankers.

Turning from routine concern with 'economic health' to long-term objectives, the remainder of the book seeks to persuade the reader of the urgent reconsideration of the place of growth in the economic policy of a technologically advanced society. The notion of economic expansion as a process on balance beneficial to humanity goes back at least a couple of centuries. About that time, however, the case for economic growth was very much stronger than it is today, not merely because we are incomparably wealthier as consumers, but also because we are increasingly subjected to the disagreeable by-products of rapid technological change. Yet so entrenched are the interests involved, commercial, institutional and scientific, and so pervasive the influence of modern communications, that economic growth has embedded itself in the ethos of our civilization. Despite the most blatant disamenities caused by the post-war economic expansion, despite the visible symptoms of a disintegrating civilization, no one today looking to advance his position to the hierarchy of government or business fails to pay homage to this sovereign concept.

II

Nearly half of this volume has been taken up with the question of spillover effects for the straightforward reason that, more than any of the other problems discussed, an increased public awareness of their nature is the pre-condition to a change in the present order of priorities, one that would enable the public to enjoy immediate and substantial benefits. The current difficulties of accurate measurement are acknowledged. But since they will exist whatever the state of the law, there are clear advantages in introducing legislation guaranteeing amenity rights to citizens. Such rights provide an equitable basis for actual compensation wherever practicable. Moreover, in view of the inevitable decision costs incurred in reaching agreement to introduce an economic improvement that modifies the application of the prevailing law among the group concerned, a weight of inertia rests on the *status quo*. The *status quo*, therefore, had better be one embracing disamenity-prohibition rather than the reverse, as at present. Furthermore, since decision costs would tend to be lower if the initiative and costs of inducing agreement within a mutually affected group lay with the creators of disamenity, anti-disamenity legislation would tend to increase the number of economic improvements that could be realized compared with the existing legislation. Finally it was pointed out that in many circumstances it is more economic, and politically more acceptable, to provide separate facilities within a given area containing people of unlike views than, instead, to enforce an optimal arrangement for the area as a whole.

In illustrating some of the chief sources of spillover, no attempt was made to disguise the author's conviction that the invention of the private automobile was one of the great disasters to have befallen the human race. Given the absence of controls, the growth of population and its increased wealth and urbanization, would in any case have produced overgrown cities. Commercial and municipal greed, coupled with architectural apathy, share the responsibility for a plethora of shabby buildings. But it needed the motor-car to consummate these developments; to fill our days with clamour and fumes, to suburbanize the countryside and to subtopianize the suburbs, and to ensure that any resort which became accessible should simultaneously become unattractive. The motor industry has come to dominate the economy almost as visibly as its products dominate the physical environment. Within a generation we have become insensitive to the growing ugliness that abounds. The common sight today of street after street strewn thick with layabout cars no longer dismays us.

The other two rapidly growing sources of disamenity used in illustrating the spread of spillover were air travel and tourism. No effective legislation putting the onus on the airlines has been contemplated by the Government. The noise created by the modern airliner is limited only by what the authorities believe people can be made to put up with. And the public may well be conditioned over time to bear with an increasing disturbance under the existing law simply (i) because of the difficulties and costs of organizing protests; (ii) because of the apparent hopelessness of prevailing upon our penny-wise authorities to put the claims of the residents before the claims of 'progress'; that is, the airlines; and (iii) because of the timidity felt by the public in pressing its claims against so effective a retort as 'the national interest'. If there is a national interest, however, our discussion establishes the case for the government's bearing the cost of its safeguard or promotion – *not* the unfortunate victims of aerial disturbance.

Certainly, the least that should be done to advance social welfare is to extend to the public some choice in so vital a matter by legislating for wholly noise-free zones – zones that are, however, desirable in all other respects, and easy of access.

As for the rapid destruction of mass tourism of the world's dwindling resources of natural beauty, a small contribution towards preservation could be made by the prohibition of motorized vehicles within selected areas and by the discontinuing of air services to such areas. Once the public becomes aware of the spread of devastation, international agreement on more radical measures may be forthcoming – if by then there is anything left worth preserving.

In sum, the thesis of the first three parts of this book is that if men are concerned primarily with human welfare, and not primarily with productivity conceived as a good in itself, they should reject economic growth as a prior aim of policy in favour of a policy of seeking to apply more selective criteria of welfare. Such a policy would involve (i) legislation recognizing the individual's right to amenity, which legislation would spearhead the attack on our post-war blight; and (ii) a substantial diversion of investible resources from industrial gadgetry to the neglected task of re-planning our towns and cities: in general, to direct our national resources and ingenuity to re-creating an environment that will gratify and inspire men.

Finally, although the enactment of amenity legislation would provide some impetus towards the creation of separate facilities, these do not depend on such legislation. Therefore, if the public could not for the present be mobilized in support of amenity rights for the citizen, any regard to the declared doctrine of increasing the range of choices available to all men must warrant an extension to existing minorities of separate facilities in matters both large and small – though especially in respect of viable areas wherein a man of moderate means may choose to dwell unmolested by those particular features of modern technology that most disturb equanimity.

III

If the moving spirit behind economic growth could speak, its motto would be: 'Enough does not suffice.' The classical description of an economic system makes sense in today's advanced economy only when stood on its head. Certainly the American economy presents us with the bizarre spectacle of growing resources pressing against limited wants. The least one can say of this phenomenon is that since consumers' wants have continuously to grow and change in response largely to the techniques of industry, the basis necessary to infer a *per capita* rise in welfare over time simply does not exist; even, that is, if human welfare were assumed to depend wholly on manufactured goods. Indeed, the rising tide of consumer goods may create as much diswelfare as welfare. The vagaries of fashion can become burdensome and the making of choices among a proliferation of models and brands can be time-consuming and disconcerting.

Once we move away from the economist's frame of reference, other factors bearing on social welfare loom large. Expanding markets in conditions of material abundance must depend upon men's dissatisfaction with their lot being perpetually renewed. Whether individual campaigns are successful or not, the institution of commercial advertising accentuates the materialistic propensities of men and promotes the view that the things which matter are the things money can buy – a view to which the young, who have plenty of need of the wherewithal if they are to avail themselves of the widely advertised opportunities for fast living and cool extravagance, are peculiarly vulnerable; a fact that explains much of their vociferous impatience and increasing violence.

These and other informal considerations were discussed at some length in Part V. Rapid technical innovation may offer to add to men's material opportunities. But it does so only by increasing the risks of their obsolescence and by therefore adding to their anxieties. Swifter means of communication have had the paradoxical effect of isolating the individual: the increased speed of transport has led to more hours commuting, a result of over-response in terms of communal spread; increased automobilization is accompanied by increased family separation; more television entails less communication between neighbours and within the family. In a word, affection and intimacy have been exchanged for travel and entertainment; the substance exchanged for the shadow.

The pursuit of efficiency in general is in fact directed towards reducing the dependence of people on one another and increasing their dependence, instead, on the machine. Indeed, by a gradual displacement of human effort from every aspect of living, technology will enable us eventually to slip through our allotted years with scarce enough sense of physical friction to be certain we are still alive.[1]

Considerations such as these that do not lend themselves to formal treatment are crucial to the issue of human welfare. And the apparent inevitability of technological change does not thereby render them irrelevant. Death too is inevitable. Yet no one feels compelled to hurry towards it on that account. Once we descry the sort of world that technology is shaping for us, it is well worth discussing whether men are likely to find it congenial or otherwise. If, on reflection, we view the prospects with misgivings we are, at least, freed from obligation to join in the ritual incantations of our patriotic growth-men. More positively, we have an additional incentive to support a policy of reducing investment in manufactures in favour of large-scale re-planning of our cities, and of preserving, restoring, and enhancing the beauty of many of our villages, towns and resorts.

[1] The recent electric-power breakdown in New York (1965), clearly to be deplored on strict grounds of efficiency, broke the spell of monotony for millions of New Yorkers. People enjoyed the shock of being thrown back on their innate resources and into sudden dependence upon one another. For a few hours at least people were freed from routine and brought together by the dark. Next door strangers spoke and gladdened to help each other. There was room for kindness.

The fault was repaired. The genie of power was returned to each home. And as the darkness brought them stumbling into each other's arms, so the hard light scattered them again.

Yet someone was quoted as saying: 'This should happen at least once a month.'

Appendix A

The Balance of Payments: 1

The substitution of government exhortation for economic policy is a feature of our national life particular to the post-war period, and though fairly popular in other countries whenever economic difficulties are encountered it has had so great a fashion in Britain that one discerns a tradition in the making. Crying wolf at the drop of an index, discovering ourselves edgily perched at the precipice every other year, lectured round the clock about our shortcomings as 'economic men' (while in between times being taken to task for our crass materialism), continually being warned that we cannot go on much longer 'living beyond our means'[1] – and yet in some mysterious manner able apparently to put off the dread day of reckoning indefinitely – it is not surprising that our responsiveness, alike to pep-talks and to crisis-talks, has waned over the years. We seem to have learned to live comfortably in an atmosphere of vague but persistent economic foreboding.

This is as well as may be. What is amiss is the common belief that the concern with growth, with inflation and with the balance of payments, is the very stuff of modern economics; furthermore, that the figures for annual productivity, interest rates, exchange reserves, are the indicators *par excellence* of our material comfort, the very substance

[1]Our current excess of imports, between £250 million and £400 million per annum, represents no more than between 1 per cent and 1½ per cent of our total national income, and well below the average per annum real increase of national income. The notion, therefore, that only hard work and austere living will enable us 'to pay our way' in the world is nonsense. It may be difficult to coax foreigners to buy that little extra of our goods that would bring us into balance, but if they were willing to buy the extra we need endure no hardship in supplying them. If not, again without hardship, we could directly reduce our excess imports or, as we shall see, invest abroad less than we have been doing.

if not the sum total of our national achievement. It is just this sort of belief that makes economics so exasperating a subject to the layman and acts over time to cramp the vision of men in authority. It is this sort of belief that imbues otherwise intelligent people with a compelling sense of urgency, so that once in office they cannot forbear to warn, to cajole and to bribe us and to threaten us about increasing this, that and the other. It is this sort of belief that prevents ministers and officials from thinking anew and critically about our existing economic institutions. For despite pop journalistic phrases about 'new thinking', 'cool looks', 'radical reorganizations', 'agonizing reappraisals', and the like, there is hardly an unorthodox idea about economics to be found lurking in the 'establishment', or for that matter in the 'anti-establishment'. Especially is this true about our notions of foreign trade.

To touch, by way of example, on a minor issue first – the connection between economic growth and the balance of payments. If we are exhorted to export more, we are no less exhorted to grow faster. More exports and more productivity are both 'good things' and, what is more, the success of either, it is believed, is promoted by the success of the other. If we grow faster we shall, we are told, improve our export position. And if we export more, this will surely enable us to grow more swiftly. We seem, therefore, to have two good reasons for keeping our attention riveted on either.

These supposed connections do not, however, stand up to cursory examination. Suppose we are so charmed with the speech of Mr Shovehard, the Minister for exports, that we all decide to abandon our private demarcation rules and, instead, to work overtime to make our goods more attractive in price and quality to the foreigners. And suppose also that we succeed thereby in reversing the present trade balance into one of a large export surplus. However, in making such goods attractive to foreigners we have also made them more plentiful and attractive to ourselves, a factor which must be chalked up to the growth account. But this increase in our exports has not *caused* the increase in growth; rather it appears as an incidental *effect* of economic growth as evinced by reduced prices and improved quality. We seem to have shown the reverse causal relationship: that growth leads to exports. This, however, is an incomplete account and we shall return to it in a moment. In the meantime, in order to effectively isolate the exports-helps-growth thesis, suppose instead that by some happy accident unforeseen by economists exports grow rapidly so that soon we are able to show a large export surplus year after year. Does this of itself promote economic growth? One reason why it may do the reverse in conditions of high employment is that while our export surplus is maintained it will be financed by an equal reduction of our available gross domestic saving and, therefore, a reduction to that extent of investment in domestic industry. Conversely, so long as an import surplus is maintained it enables us to release domestic resources in order to add to the new investment already made available by domestic saving. Economic analysis can go further than this, of course, but enough has been said to suggest that a statement that economic growth is itself helped along by an expansion of exports is not a self-evident piece of reasoning.

As for the reverse relation: that of economic growth stimulating exports, although the assertion has a superficial plausibility – as, for instance, in the first half of the above paragraph – this relation, too, tends to wilt under scrutiny. The effects on our balance of payments of an increase in the rate of economic growth may be considered under two main headings (1) the aggregative, and (2) the technological. Under (1) we include two general propositions: (*a*) inasmuch as this country spends a given fraction of its income on imports, a faster growth of its real income from any cause – increasing population, increasing *per capita* income with, or without, technological advance – results in a faster growth of its imports from the rest of the world. (*b*) In so far as the level of our prices rises compared with the price-levels of other countries this fraction of our income spent on imports itself tends to rise (and the fraction the world spends on our exports to fall), thus aggravating further an adverse balance of payments. And our price-level may well rise, both absolutely and relative to world prices, if the increase in our rate of growth is accompanied by attempts to push further into our 'full-employment zone'.

Under (2) we take account of the effects of improved technology on the prices of our import substitutes and on the prices of our exports. (*a*) If the spurt in productivity chiefly takes the form of innovations in the domestic production of new or cheaper substitutes for our imports, the volume and the value of our imports are thereby reduced. (*b*) On the other hand, if our productivity advances are concentrated in our export industries, then although the *volume* of our exports will tend to increase, their *value* will increase only if, despite our lower prices, foreigners spend more of their currency on them. Should they spend less on them (increasing their purchases by a proportion that is smaller than the fall in our prices) the value of our exports will fall.

As it happens, the quantitative information necessary to strike a balance of tendency for the UK is, as yet, unavailable. Until it becomes available there can be no acceptable presumption that, in general, a faster rate of economic growth in the UK would improve the balance-of-payments position. In the meantime, however, it is my guess that it would be likely to worsen the balance-of-payments.

Let us then turn to a more fundamental problem, the importance to our economy of a large volume of trade. The public, long-conditioned by their newspapers, are in no doubt that we must export to 'survive'. If we have managed to survive for so long without exporting enough to 'pay our way' in the world, it is presumably because the world has been lenient with us so far. The transition from export-mindedness to mercantilism is, however, short and easy. It is not uncommon for large export orders, gained or lost, to make front-page news. Apparently goods exported emit an odour of sanctity denied to common or garden goods that remain to be consumed inside the country. The impression persists that by exporting we pile up reserves of economic strength along with foreign currencies, and that by importing we dissipate them. An announcement from the Board of Trade that the country's exports are breaking all records has a regenerative effect on our spirits: we begin to feel proud, confident and very respectable. One dares not imagine the general acclaim and exhilaration that would follow the discovery, at the end of the year, that we had in fact exported the whole of our national output.

Now businessmen need seldom trouble to push their ideas to their logical conclusions. They know that more of some things is good and more of other things is bad. Without a shadow of doubt, exports are one of the good things: it follows that we cannot really have enough of them. The trained economist, however, has at the fore of his mind the notion of an 'optimum' quantity or flow of things. The 'optimum' volume of trade would be the 'just right' volume more than which, or less, is to be avoided. Though this concept is straightforward enough, owing to a highly volatile economic environment this optimum volume of foreign trade is practically impossible to measure with a pretence of anything approaching exactness. For all that, the notion of an optimum volume of trade as a goal of attainment could with advantage replace the current mercantilist view rampant among businessmen, journalists and politicians. It would increase their receptiveness to the possibility, the likelihood even, that the volume of our foreign trade is too large; that we should be more comfortable with a smaller volume of trade.

It is not necessary in this essay, however, to burden the reader with the theory of optimal tariffs which demonstrates that, starting from a free trade equilibrium there exists a set of tariffs that (in the absence of retaliation) would enable the community to exploit the maximum advantage from its foreign trade and, in any case, attain a higher level of potential welfare than would exist in a completely free trade situation. Nevertheless, by translating into welfare terms the two related effects of a tariff – a reduction in the total purchases of imports and the consequent improvement in the terms of trade – such theorems do serve to combat parochial doctrine about the advantages of increasing foreign trade.

In the existing circumstances, however, it is yet more relevant to consider ways of reducing the volume of imports, and of stabilizing its composition, with the object simply of diminishing the magnitude and recurrence of balance-of-payment crises in a world of fixed exchange rates. A discussion of this possibility has the incidental merit of exposing in another crucial context the falseness of the no-choice myth. There are no 'musts' in international trade, as in fact there are none in the field of economic policy. 'Export or perish' slogans are a misleading form of rhetoric. Economics is concerned, *inter alia*, with investigating the implications of *alternative* choices that are open to us. And if presumably honest men talk to us as if there is in fact no choice, they do so either in ignorance of the opportunities that are open to us or else from the conviction – which occasionally, at least, ought to be made explicit – that we should concur with them in rejecting all the alternatives did we but know them.

Turning, therefore, to the volume of foreign trade, we might begin by agreeing that, given the already outsize population of these islands, there would be genuine hardship for a long time if we could not import some minimum assortment of goods from abroad. Whatever our conception of this minimum assortment, once we extend the import ration from this bare minimum we move out of the range of discomfort and enter a range of diminishing frustration. The ration now includes goods that are generally admitted to be highly desirable. We move on from there to include the range of fashion and luxury goods: French cheeses,

Italian shoes, German cars, Belgian chocolate, American cigarettes, Japanese toys, Dutch tomatoes, and so on; things not to be spurned, and important for a variety of reasons to some people, but which could be called 'essential' only by a misleading use of language. Yet if a sizeable proportion of our import bill does consist of goods such as these that cannot reasonably be classified as 'essential', and indeed may more usefully be classified as 'expendable', it is surely perverse that responsible ministers should continue to exhort us as though such imports were a matter of life and death to our economy. Of course, they do not say this in so many words; rather they talk about the country's need to *export*, and labour us with patriotic duty to strain to the utmost to sell abroad. But the additional exports we must strain ourselves to sell can be properly regarded as 'essential' to our 'solvency' only in so far as our imports of close substitutes and luxuries and quasi-luxuries are themselves essential.[1]

Ordinary honesty should make it clear to the public that we have, for one reason or another, adopted the policy of allowing the import of 'expendable' goods and, in consequence, we are now seemingly up against the wall trying, at the given rate of exchange, to pay for them with exports. For all I know such a policy if understood by the public might be universally approved – another challenge, perhaps! But since these simple implications of our current foreign trade policy are never put to the public in this candid fashion, we have no means of knowing what the response of the public would be.[2]

One of the things that we import to the tune of some £300 million a year (taking an average over the last six years) that cannot by any stretch of imagination be called essential is foreign securities[3] – in other

---

[1] In general, it is misleading to assert that we *need* to export, say, an additional £200 million in order to meet the excess of our imports unless it is agreed that *everything* we import is *needed* in that same sense.

[2] While it is true that we have certain international commitments and that unilateral action of some sorts and on some scale would invite retaliation, there is no reason to speak and act as though we were tied hand and foot by the rest of the world, and unable to move a joint save by international consensus. It is possible that the continuance of our traditional policies carries more depressing consequences than those that would follow our opting out of international agreements (if necessary). However, as we shall see, there are other, more radical choices yet available to us.

[3] It is true that the import of securities may lead to export orders. But the fraction of exports thereby generated qualifies the magnitude only, not the essential argument.

words, lending abroad or the export of capital.[1] Moreover, this is one kind of import which, if curtailed, is not in the least likely to cause reprisals.

In addition, there are longer term allocative implications that suggest a reduction of our capital exports, at least if we are concerned with the economic position of the domestic economy.[2] It may well be that the British investor's immediate expectations are realized and he obtains a higher return from his capital abroad than he does by investing it in the home economy. However, as additional capital is exported its yield abroad diminishes. In general this causes the yield on all the intra-marginal units of capital, already exported, to diminish also. Thus, the net return to a marginal unit of capital is less than what is received by the investor of that marginal unit by an amount equal to the fall in the return on all previously exported units of capital. Indeed, the net return to the domestic economy of the additional unit of capital exported might well be negative.[3]

There are two other reasons why investment abroad tends to be too high relative to domestic investment. The first arises from the process of innovation. In so far as technologically more advanced capital equipment is introduced in the production of specific goods the prices of such goods (relative to other goods and relative to wages) tend to fall. As a result, the return on any previous investment of now-obsolescent capital also tends to fall. The investor is aware of this risk of obsolescence but is indifferent to incurring the risk at home or abroad. But the domestic economy ought not to be indifferent. Within the domestic economy such losses suffered by the domestic investor represent a

---

[1] Any interest or dividends collected in this country over the future do feature as part of our invisible exports. They must therefore be taken into account in any long-term policy. But we are concerned here with the immediate and short-term balance of payments problem.

[2] If, on the other hand, we are concerned quite selflessly with the welfare of the world at large, we should seek to increase international factor mobility – encouraging the export of our capital especially to underdeveloped countries and importing their labour – until some international equilibrium is reached.

[3] For the world economy as a whole this reduction in the returns of all intra-marginal units represents a transfer from the owners of capital to the rest of the population. But from the standpoint of the capital-exporting country, the fall in the return on the intra-marginal units of capital already exported is to be regarded as an 'external diseconomy'. For the additional investor unwittingly inflicts a loss on all the existing holders of foreign capital. Such a loss would be taken into account only if the export of capital were in the hands of a monopoly.

gain for the domestic population. If, on the other hand, the investment is placed abroad, any such subsequent loss represents a transfer from the domestic capitalist to the foreign population.

The third reason for the tendency to over-invest abroad arises from institutional factors. The rational investor compares the returns to his investment at home and abroad net of all taxes. Now the return to the British economy of an increment of investment abroad is in fact no more than the return received by the British investor after paying taxes to the foreign government. The return to the British economy of investment at home, on the other hand, exceeds the net return received by the British investor by the amount of the tax he pays to the British Government.

The case for the control of foreign investment is even stronger than these long-term considerations suggest, when such investment is seen against the backcloth of continual balance-of-payments difficulties. For this search by investors for larger profits abroad is what ultimately contributes to bringing about the credit restrictions at home, to say nothing of our government having to borrow abroad, on short term, at very high rates.[1]

Another practical way of reducing our imports is to grow more of our foodstuffs at home. Increased self-sufficiency in foodstuffs (after allowance for the import-content of increased home production) may save us well over £100 million of imports and, possibly, without much increase in costs. Farming is one of Britain's more efficient industries, and if there were some initial rise in costs it would probably be absorbed within a few years. In the short run, moreover, import restrictions might well lower the foreign price of our remaining food imports since some time must elapse before foreign supplies find other suitable outlets.

Finally, as one looks down the list of items imported into, and exported from, the UK, one is invariably struck by the close resemblance between them. Textiles, clothing, footwear, hardware, automobiles, ships, trucks, aircraft, paints, machinery of all kinds, cameras, toys and vast quantities of chemicals are both imported and exported. One

---

[1] It does not follow from these remarks that no foreign investment should be permitted; merely that the bulk of our foreign lending should not be determined by the profit expectations of investors, but rather by more comprehensive welfare criteria and/or by considerations bearing on the country's long-term economic policy.

could reasonably surmise that a large proportion of these things, in particular the finished goods, are very close substitutes, and that although their further restriction might cause some occasional resentment – and would certainly incur the charge of retrograde among the doctrinaire – it would not be likely to inflict hardship.[1] At any rate, increased restrictions on these luxuries, quasi-luxuries, and close substitutes would, in the immediate short run at least, reduce the apparent need to whip ourselves into 'viability'. However, this proposal to examine ways and means of reducing our present import bill, it should be stressed, is not for the purpose of gaining any ephemeral trade advantage. True, the immediate effect of implementing the proposed measures might be regarded as an attempt to cut our foreign purchases to what we could comfortably afford, and as such one need not alarm oneself with exaggerated expectations of retaliation. But the larger objective is to reduce permanently the volume of our foreign trade and, perhaps, to induce other Western European countries to do the same. By eliminating much – just how much can be left to discussion – of the trade in luxuries, close substitutes and such goods as one might reasonably classify as expendable, one could hope for greater stability in the pattern and volume of trade over the future. One might hope therefore to check the present trend towards an increasingly fluctuating pattern of foreign trade, especially as by far the greater part of world trade takes place between the affluent countries of the West, and as a proportion of world trade, is increasing. On the supply side, more rapidly advancing technology entails a swifter shifting to and fro of short-lived technological advantage in closely competitive products – and, with larger productive units, the competition is likely to be pretty ruthless. On the demand side, as the margin for non-essentials grows over the future, one may surely anticipate more impulse- and fashion-buying, features that can only aggravate the increasing vicissitudes of international trade. Of course, there will always be those who view the fierce competitive struggle with exhilaration. To others, who see in life more serious objectives than a perpetual jockeying for position, the opportunity of permanently reducing the least stable, or most expendable, components of our imports by some sacrifice of variety and

---

[1] I would say that not less than £800 million of our yearly imports come into this category.

perhaps cheapness, in order to remain free from perpetual anxiety, may have a stronger appeal.[1]

---

[1] It will always be argued by the inveterate free trader that the competition of such foreign goods, whether Italian Fiats, or French frocks, helps to keep down domestic prices. However, the size of the British home market alone is, for practically all of those sorts of imports, large enough to exploit fully the economies of scale. Where the efficient plant size is small enough it is up to the Government to make much more use of the Monopolies Commission and the Restrictive Practices Court in promoting competition. Where not, product standardization, either voluntary or government-inspired, may enable us to reduce costs without much sacrifice – or, indeed, with some welcome sacrifice – of variety.

The Balance of Payments: 2

When one bears in mind the disproportionate influence exerted by foreign trade in our domestic affairs, and the absorption of time and financial talent in the endless task of 'maintaining the strength of the pound', one is tempted to suggest measures that are more radical yet than a deliberate reduction in our volume of trade. It is surely worth paying a high price in order to end once and for all time this perverse phenomenon of the foreign-trade tail wagging the domestic economy. Indeed, it would be an act of emancipation, if not of mercy, to free successive governments from unceasing preoccupation with the balance of payments and thus to provide them with the time and breathing space necessary to look around and discover what is happening to the country.

Two alternative policies to the present system which could contribute substantially to this desideratum are (*a*) state-trading, and (*b*) a freely flexible pound, proposals that can be expected with confidence to meet with a dusty reception from the Press if only for the reason that either treads heavily on material, intellectual and ideological interests. None the less, if we are to take seriously the popular slogan about 'facing up to the twentieth century' both are worthy of more public attention than they receive.

I use the term state-trading reluctantly, aware of the antagonism it arouses in the breasts of those who equate personal freedom with the operation of free markets and perceive sinister possibilities in any extension of state enterprise. Yet no more is intended here than the establishment of a state-trading agency with powers to enter into long-term contracts with other countries (on a bilateral or multilateral basis) in order to ensure the means of paying for adequate supplies, in some sense, of foodstuffs, raw materials and other 'priority' goods. Such an agency would adopt some method for appointing domestic firms to meet its long-term export contracts and some method (possibly auctioning) of disposing of its imports to domestic wholesalers. One may reasonably assume, in addition, that there would still be frequent opportunities for supplementing the variety of imports by further bargains between countries.

This is not the place to develop a detailed description of the operation of such an agency, nor to defend it against the familiar objections – the rigidity and ponderousness of such public agencies in contrast to the alleged flexibility and variety of the existing private enterprise system. Indeed, one would be pleasantly surprised if such a state body managed entirely to escape such defects. But such ponderousness, if it were irreducible, would be acknowledged as part of the price we should be willing to pay in order to unchain our domestic economic policy from the inescapable vagaries of unhindered privately conducted trade at fixed exchange rates.

It is to be understood that such an agency should for the most part confine its long-term contracts to ensuring 'essential' imports, with the option of shopping around for bargains in the less essential goods. The import of additional 'luxury' goods might also be allowed by selling in a free market any excess of foreign earnings. This possibility brings us to the other proposal: the attempt to establish a freely fluctuating pound – the price of the pound, in terms of foreign currencies, moving continually so as to equate the demand for sterling (in exchange for foreign currencies) with its current supply, irrespective of the domestic policy the Government chooses to pursue.

Under such an institution the Government *need* no longer hold reserves of gold of foreign currencies,[1] for it has no obligation to maintain the price of sterling on world markets. And no consideration of an external balance can prevent it, at all times, from pursuing the monetary and fiscal policy that seems appropriate to the domestic

---

[1] Though the Government does not need to hold any reserves, there is much to be said for the Government's continuing, for several years, to use exchange reserves to iron out random, seasonal, and other irrelevant exchange fluctuations that might occur during a transitional period during which the foreign exchange market was growing in the expertise and resources necessary to free the Government completely from further concern with the exchange rate.

situation.[1] In principle, the mechanism is simple: if at the existing exchange rate our demand for foreign currency persistently exceeds foreigners' demand for our currency, the value of the pound would tend to fall, and would continue to fall until – our goods having become cheaper in terms of foreigners' currencies (and foreign goods having become dearer in terms of sterling) – equilibrium is restored.[2]

Although our experience of flexible exchange rates is very limited there is nothing in the brief British experience – between 1919 and 1924 and again from 1931, when we were forced off gold by panic flights of capital, until the Tripartite Pact of 1936 – or in the recent Canadian experience, between 1950 and 1962 (during which period, although the Canadian dollar was nominally free to float, the Government intervened to 'smooth out' erratic movements), which gives ground for the oft-voiced suspicion that a freely floating pound would be unstable; that is, the exchange rate would fluctuate so wildly as to seriously damage the international exchange of goods. Nor does this limited experience provide any evidence for the view that a flexible exchange rate, of itself, is likely to impart an inflationary momentum to the economy.

To those wedded to the *status quo*, every conceivable misadventure associated with a radical change of policy is depicted as though it were a

[1]The existence of some £4 billion sterling balances held by foreigners, the greater part by governments, clearly poses a problem. But a problem would have to be very many times more difficult than this for it to weigh as a serious objection against so far-reaching an experiment. Obviously, some arrangement involving, say, an exchange guarantee would have to be reached with the chief countries holding sterling balances in order to avoid, during the first few years of the experiment, any prolonged downward pressure on the pound arising from the efforts of large holders of sterling to convert their holdings into other currencies.

[2]The greater part of our demand for foreign currencies arises, of course, from our demand for foreign goods and services. The less responsive is our demand for imports and the less responsive is the foreign demand for our exports, with respect to movements in the rate of exchange, the larger the required change in the price of sterling for any autonomous shift in demand. There has always been much controversy over the actual degree of responsiveness of imports and exports to changes in the exchange rates. Attempts to estimate the elasticity of foreign demand for the goods of any particular country have not brought agreement any closer. It must be admitted, however, that the less responsive are these demands the more difficult will the scheme be to work. If there were good reasons to believe that very large movements of the exchange rate had little effect on the respective demands for currency, one would tend to favour state-trading in 'essentials', leaving the less essentials and 'luxuries' to free exchanges, since for these latter goods price-responsiveness is generally believed to be high.

veritable certainty, while the encumbrances daily inflicted upon us by the existing policy are barely mentioned. The hypothetical dangers[1] are thus highly overrated compared with the quite certain and palpable disadvantages of maintaining a fixed exchange rate in a world which can look increasingly to more rapid shiftings of the pattern of international trade. Moreoever, neither of the contingencies feared, allowing they took place, are so dangerous as to prohibit some experiment along these lines. No matter what the uncertainty surrounding the future movements of the pound, it is hardly likely that the volume of trade would be much reduced since it will always be open to traders to hedge against risks by selling or buying foreign exchange in organized forward exchange markets.[2]

As for the instability of a freely moving exchange rate, if we mean by that term wide fluctuations within short periods, the likelihood is greater: (1) the greater the proportion of the total transactions in the currency is for speculative purposes as distinct from trading purposes,[3] (2) the more volatile and erratic are the expectations of speculators,[4] and (3) the less responsive is the direction of trade to changes in the

---

[1] Two other popular objections to flexible exchange rates may be worth mentioning:

(1) Since forward markets are limited to short-term transactions, there would be no institutional mechanisms to cover exchange risks incurred by long-term foreign investment which might, therefore, start to fall off. However, an addition of, say, one per cent per annum extra return on a fifteen to twenty-five-year investment would be more than enough to compensate for the risk of very large changes in the rate of exchange.

(2) Flexible exchange rates, it is alleged, may cause fluctuations in the foreign demand for the products of our export industries so reducing their efficient growth. However, this contingency must be compared with their fate under a rigid pound backed by relatively low exchange reserves. The resulting 'stop-go' policies with which we are familiar, are yet more damaging since they affect not merely the export industries but practically all industries in the economy.

[2] Not, of course, that it would matter much if the volume of trade were somewhat reduced. The essentials in trade would easily weather any residual uncertainty, which uncertainty would have more of a damping effect on the import of 'expendables' – goods having a relatively high elasticity of import demand and a relatively low 'welfare content'.

[3] This is a functional distinction, since to some extent the exporter, or importer, is, or may become, a speculator.

[4] In general, all price expectations may be regarded as destabilizing within limits (a rise in price, for instance, leading to expectations of a further rise in price) and stabilizing outside these limits (a rise in price leading to expectations that the price will return to a lower level). The wider these limits the more destabilizing are expectations.

value of the currency. Much therefore depends upon the 'real' forces – the response of our imports and exports to a change in the international value of the pound – and the organization of the foreign exchange market. Stability increases according to the size of the market for foreign exchange, the accuracy of the information at its disposal, and the ability of professional speculators to forecast correctly. Although, as indicated, the historical experience on which any sober judgement of the likely course of events is lacking, two considerations seem to augur well for the experiment. First, existing commodity markets have served the community well: it is generally believed that in their absence commodity prices would fluctuate more steeply than they do. Of course prices fluctuate sharply enough even on such well organized markets, but this is unavoidable since the supply of the crop is usually fixed by the harvest for some time, and also because the ultimate demand for it is usually highly inelastic. These conditions are not present in international trade and one may reasonably expect that proportional fluctuations will be less. Secondly, fears of wild fluctuations, as also fears of continued decline in the international value of the pound[1] should

---

[1] Though much is made of the possibility of a 'ratchet effect' – a wage cost inflation taking place whenever the value of the pound fell and import prices rose, with no symmetrical reduction of wages when the pound rose and import prices fell – it is difficult to believe that the day-to-day fluctuations of the exchange would have that much impact on the cost-of-living index, which would rise noticeably only if there were a persistent trend against the pound. Even so we must remember that a 4–5 per cent rise in the cost of living maintained over a year or so and caused only by imports would require an average rise in their prices of over 20 per cent.

There are two main reasons why import prices could rise appreciably. For structural reasons: e.g. a rise in the UK demand for certain types of foreign goods (because of a change in taste), or a long-term reduction in foreign supplies, will lower the value of the freely fluctuating pound. The consequent rise in import prices under these circumstances would, however, also take place under fixed exchange rates. The other reason for rising import prices is the general substitution of foreign goods for British goods as a consequence of an already existing inflation in the UK. Whereas with a fixed exchange rate rising domestic prices cause a switch of demand from domestic goods for foreign goods thereby generating an import surplus, which enables us to pass on to other countries some of our inflationary pressure, flexible exchange rates act instead to contain the domestic inflation by causing the prices of foreign goods to rise along with those of our domestic goods. However, if we cannot 'export' some of our inflation, neither can we 'import' any – the insulation works both ways, and to that extent puts the burden of domestic policy where it should rightly be, entirely on the domestic economy.

Obviously, then, a policy of flexible exchange rates does not of itself promote price-stability. If industries are willing and, as a result of the Government's

be brought into relation with the fact that at least there is no need for these things. We have, after all, been able to maintain a quite rigid exchange rate for some sixteen years without apparent calamity. Stresses and strains there have been, and some trying moments also. But the stark fact that we have been able to continue without any change at all in the exchange rate for sixteen years strongly suggests that large and frequent changes are not necessary. Much, however, depends upon the way we make the transition to free exchanges. Thus, granted that setting up a free market in foreign currencies would be a much larger undertaking than setting up an organized commodity market, one should be able to count on the Government's initial support of the experiment, first by launching the venture when the pound was fairly strong and, secondly, by using its existing reserves to iron out the wilder speculative movements until such time as the market grew in skill and resources and was able to stand comfortably on its own feet.

The fears of strong speculative pressure are in fact a legacy not of a period of flexible exchanges but of a period of pegged exchange rates which, by providing any amateur with plenty of time to observe events, consult the obvious figures, and ponder the degree of unanimity of the experts, veritably invites the non-specialized public to take up a safe option. If a balance-of-payments deficit continues to use up exchange reserves for several consecutive years to the manifest concern of the Government, one stands to lose very little by selling sterling, spot or forward, if the pound is not depreciated, and to gain a great deal if, after all, it is depreciated. These one-way options, a boon to ordinary businessmen and a curse to governments trying to maintain pegged rates, cannot without the strictest capital controls be dissociated from a system of fixed exchange rates. The relevant generalization, in fact, is: the higher the degree of exchange flexibility the smaller the opportunity for the parasitic speculation that is such a pronounced feature of the system of fixed exchanges.

At this stage, one should recognize the more cautious proposals that are put forward from time to time to ease us away from the rigidly fixed

ineffectual monetary policy, able, to make continued concessions to the unions in the belief that, in times of creeping inflation, higher prices are easily passed on to the public, a change to flexible exchange rates will not suffice to alter this entrepreneurial behaviour. However, just because we can no longer run into debt and head for a balance of payments crisis, the consequences of ineffectual monetary policy are immediate and wholly visible.

exchange rate; for instance, that the degree of flexibility of the pound should be limited to a rise or fall of 2 per cent per annum, in effect limiting the movement of the pound to a maximum of 4 per cent within a year, a maximum speculative gain that could, if necessary, be offset by a differential in the interest rates between this country and others. Such proposals move in the right direction[1] and would be an improvement over the present system in giving some increased flexibility to domestic policy. But only as we move on to the bolder scheme of complete flexibility do we confer independence on our domestic economic policy.[2]

Although much has been written on this question of exchange rate flexibility the conclusions reached have always been much influenced by basic ideologies and one's estimates of political 'realities' – which estimates sometimes go with a strong preference for inertia as against initiative and experiment. An unbroken period of fixed exchange rates with all the day-to-day, week-to-week and year-to-year preoccupation with these thorny, albeit familiar, problems about stock-piling, seasonal variations, 'leads and lags', the movements of gold and the exchange reserves, foreign confidence and central-bank co-operation, to say nothing of a succession of international conferences with endless proposals for increasing international liquidity and expanding international trade, all this has created stubborn material and intellectual interests. The cumulated weight of years of habitual response lies heavy on our spirit, and though our political leaders follow the fashion and croak 'challenge' from time to time there has been no response in terms of

[1]This 'wider band' proposal and/or a 'sliding parity' (allowing a discretion to any country, under revised I M F rules, to change the rate of exchange by, say, one-sixth of one per cent each month if a deficit, or a surplus, continues to appear) among other proposals have been briefly discussed by Professor J. E. Meade in two articles (*The Three Banks Review*, September 1964 and June 1966). The one serious objection there is to the wide band proposal is that, in order to avoid speculative pressure against the currency of the deficit country, interest rate differentials as between the deficit and surplus countries must be such as to offset potential speculative gains. Since the deficit country has to raise its short-term interest rates in these circumstances it is denied the free use of the one weapon that it should be making more use of in pursuit of a domestic policy of full employment with price stability.

[2]While it is true that changes in the direction of international trade may affect the domestic price level, and also that changes in domestic policy may affect the pattern of international trade, even with a system of flexible exchange rates, under such a system the Government *need* concentrate only on domestic policy.

political ingenuity. For the recurring ailment nothing but more of the same old medicine: sweat, toil and exhortations to export.

The aim of this brief discussion has been limited to persuading readers of the habitual magnification of the balance-of-payments problem and the error residing in the conventional belief that we have no choice at all but to export or go under in a world in which some sort of critical 'race' is on, one from which we cannot hope to escape. In the following pages we make no further reference to international trade, not because there are no incidental balance-of-payments effects flowing from one sort of domestic policy as against some other, but because the crux of the balance-of-payments problem, as seen here, is the psychological one of being unable to break free from long-established habits of thought. Until we are ready to dare to think unorthodox thoughts we must dismiss as illusory any hope of being able, permanently, to emancipate domestic policy from the vicissitude of international trade and capital movements.

Economic Growth and National Defence

In public debates on foreign policy it is obviously indiscreet to draw a clear distinction between naked self-interest and moral obligation, and between expedience and principle. It is no less foolish in private to ignore or blur the distinctions – as we frequently do when deciding policy on critical issues, such as immigration or relations with the Arab states, by invoking the comfortable doctrine that by helping others we ultimately help ourselves. However that be, since it is the *need* for faster economic growth that is at issue here, only naked self-interest concerns us.

For historical reasons it has come to be thought that the security of nations is strengthened by their 'sphere of influence' abroad. The idea has been extended to a popular presumption that the West is strengthened against the menace of Communism by the spread of democratic régimes in the 'uncommitted' countries. Investing a larger area of the map with a greater significance than a smaller, and deriving assurance from the area being shaded the right colour, are habits we are only beginning to overcome. But the fact is that the West – the English speaking countries plus Western Europe – could, with slight material inconvenience, sever themselves economically and politically from the rest of the world. It could form a compact trade and development bloc and leave all other countries to their own devices. True, the Communists might start taking over every country in Asia, Africa and South America. But far from this development being a threat to the West, it would be more likely to bring China and Russia into collision. More certainly, it would keep the Communist powers, when not in conflict, fully occupied for decades struggling to assimilate hundreds of millions of initially unwilling subjects.

Military power today depends very little on land mass or on numbers. It depends on technology and the industrial base that serves it. The overwhelming superiority of the West in these respects would be strengthened by its closer integration. The spread of communist control over a wide variety of people living in the poorer areas of the world would, on the other hand, tend to over-extend and dissipate its resources.

Accepting this much brings us to the critical question: in order to maintain the superiority of our war technology, must the West not seek to maintain its rate of economic growth? As a particular example, if we wish to keep abreast of aero-technology should we not promote civil aviation?

A belief that we should act in this way may have been excusable in earlier times when technology was relatively primitive and innovation was a by-product of the spread of enterprise and the growth of the market. Today, in contrast, technological innovation is increasingly a product of highly organized scientific research. Any notion that the encouragement of, say, civil aviation is necessary in the interests of air defence is a myth. In Britain, for example, resources devoted to research in aircraft technology could be maintained, indeed expanded, while simultaneously withdrawing all resources currently expended in operating commercial airlines.

In more general terms, a policy based on the premise that 'all is grist to the mill' and – since everything in the economy depends on everything else – only the promotion of growth in general provides the necessary circumstance for satisfactory progress in any one or more priority sectors cannot be seriously defended. It is in fact the antithesis of economic efficiency. If we are anxious to improve our conventional war technology, we should be ill-advised to subsidize air-pistols or fireworks, or promote automobile sales, or give economic privileges to the oil companies. It is incomparably less expensive to direct scientific research towards the specific ends desired. And a government disposing annually of over two billion pounds on military defence can afford to build its own optimal-sized plants for specific armaments and to organize research on any desired scale. It need be in no way dependent on the research undertaken by particular industries and, therefore, in no way dependent upon the size of the growth rates of such industries.

Interpretation of the Benefits of Private Transport

I

Let us construct hypothetical situations to reveal some of the circumstances under which 'consumer's surplus', when used as a money index of the benefits derived from private automobile travel, give perverse results – a rise in the index being accompanied by a reduction in the benefit experienced by the motorist. Less surprisingly, it will also be shown that the use of this index in determining optimal traffic flows, in benefit-cost studies, and in estimating rates of return on road investment, results in over-investment in road construction unless the alternatives to private automobile travel are properly priced.

We shall define consumer's surplus (CS) here as the maximum sum the individual is prepared to pay in order to secure a permit to buy a car at the market price, given his expectation of re-selling it for a known sum after having motored M miles. And although not essential, it will simplify the analysis to assume (1) that in all sectors of a fully-employed economy, except those under examination, price is already equal to social marginal cost, and (2), provisionally at least, that there are no spillover effects external to the transport industry which affect the amenity of the public.

Phase I of the situation is one in which there is no private traffic, an efficient system of public transport, say a bus service, linking together all parts of the city. Individual A, typical of others, uses the bus daily to take him to the centre of the city in about ten minutes. Public transport is also used for his occasional outings.

Phase II is the transitional one in which A buys a new car that, in the circumstances prevailing (which he, short-sightedly, projects into the future) is expected to take him to the centre in five minutes. On his anticipations of the future he makes a C S of, say £800. Provided that only A buys a car, and nothing else changes, A is to that extent better off in the I I Phase than in the I Phase.

Phase I I I occurs after a large enough number of others follow A's example. Within two or three years, we may suppose, the increase in the number of private cars is such that it takes A fifteen minutes to drive to work. He realizes now that he was better off in Phase I, but this opportunity is now closed to him. For owing to the build-up of private traffic the congestion is such that it would take him twenty-five minutes to reach his office by bus. Moreoever, since bus drivers have had to be compensated for the increased difficulties and risk of driving, the bus fare has risen.

Phase I I I' is the situation which exists when public transport has been withdrawn altogether, as may happen if commercial considerations alone prevail. Analytically, however, it differs from I I I only in being a more extreme case of it.

II

By assumption A is now worse off in Phase I I I than he was in I. He would, of course, prefer I I to either I I I or I. But I I is a transitional phase only: it is no longer open to him, and could be reserved for him only if he exercised the powers of a dictator.

Since A is typical of other individuals who have changed from being passengers to being motorists, we can assume that I is *socially* preferred to I I I. Dealers in motor-cars and accessories may, themselves, be on balance better off, but we suppose that they could not compensate the rest of the community and remain as well off as they were in I.

There are two things to notice: first, that under existing institutions there are no self-generating forces that can restore to the community the socially preferred Phase I. Only a collective decision could return the community from the existing I I I or I I I' phase to the original I situation. Second, that A's C S on his automobile in the I I I Phase will exceed that in the I I Phase, notwithstanding that he gets less benefit from his automobile in the I I I Phase. It was, in fact, just because public transport was so cheap and efficient in the I Phase that the maximum amount he was prepared to pay for successive miles of private driving was lower than it was in the I I I Phase, where the public transport

alternative was unattractive. If now, for example, we move to the III'
Phase in which the public transport alternative is completely withdrawn,
a loss of welfare will certainly be experienced by the remaining passengers. Some of these ex-passengers will have little choice but to
purchase automobiles. Compared with their new alternatives, of either
walking to work or not working in the city, the CS on their purchases
will be positive, and may even be large. Since we may assume that the
cars used by the displaced passengers in the III' Phase take up more
road space than did the displaced buses, the motorists in the III' Phase,
of which A was a typical member, will also be worse off than they were
in III.

If the benefit conferred by the private automobile on its owner is
measured by his CS, or any proxy measure, the chronological change
through II, III and III' will appear to register a continuously increasing benefit notwithstanding the continuous deterioration in his welfare
in this respect.

A similar development could of course arise in other situations, for
instance in a suburb linked by rail to the city. At the given rail fare n
commuters are required in order for the railway to 'break even'. If,
therefore, owing to an initial change from rail to road, only m commuters
remain $(m < n)$, the railway service must close down. The closure
clearly makes the m commuters worse off. But it also makes those who
were, before the closure, travelling by private automobile worse off (a)
because m commuters now have to travel by road and increase the congestion there; and (b) because even though automobile travellers made
no use of the railway, or used it infrequently, it did provide a form of
insurance in the case of the car being out of service – or for such
occasions when, for one reason or another, the motorist did not feel up
to driving.

Again, however, despite the fact that everyone going into the city is
adversely affected by the railway closure, the community's demand for
road travel will be seen to have expanded and the individual and,
therefore, the collective consumers' surplus of automobile owners will
reveal a gain. Each ex train-commuter who has now perforce to purchase an automobile must reveal a positive CS. As for the remainder,
once the railway service has been removed the only alternative, we may
suppose, is walking to the city. The maximum amount any individual
would be willing to pay for the ith journey by car is consequently greater.

III

These simple illustrations may serve to remind the transport expert that there are difficulties other than those of statistical measurement. Not only can the index of consumers' benefit rise over time without any actual experience of benefit – simply because 'real' income is increasing, and therefore people are prepared to pay more for the ith unit of any good, or service, whose actual utility to them in fact remains unchanged – but such an index can rise concurrently with an actual reduction of benefit. The more significant parts of the *ceteris paribus* of all consumer's surplus (and rent) analysis relate to the constancy of the prices, and/or availabilities of, the close substitutes, and complements, for the good or service in question. The more effective the good y as, say, a substitute for x, the smaller will be the consumer's surplus on purchases of x at the given prices. Raise the price of y, and ultimately withdraw it from the market, and this simultaneously *reduces* the welfare of the consumer and *increases* his measure of consumer's surplus on purchases of x.

The same illustrations also serve to show that any allocative recommendations flowing from such estimates of the demand curve for automobile travel are invalid in the absence of optimal outputs in the alternative services. In the first illustration, as the community moves into Phase III the transport expert may continue to revise upward his estimate of the 'optimal traffic flow' which expands, therefore, along with the fall in motorists' welfare. Of course, in the event of Phase III' being reached, there remaining no alternative but to walk to work, the elasticity of demand may be so low as to make little difference, if any, between the actual traffic flow and the optimal traffic flow.

The transport expert may also use the data in III and III' to justify investment in road-widening, in fly-overs, freeways and bridges, in the attempt to accommodate the expanding number of private automobiles.

Now if there were effective methods for imputing congestion costs in the first place, other recommendations would follow which, under our assumption that in all other sectors price was equal to social marginal cost, could be justified. Beginning with a satisfactory public transport in Phase I, such a mechanism would require that full compensation for any inconvenience caused to every passenger and bus driver by the marginal car be imputed to the marginal car. Such a scheme would ensure that no additional car be allowed on the route(s) in question unless it were able to effect a Pareto improvement – the owner of the car being at least no worse off after compensating everyone else using the roads – bus passengers, bus drivers, and intra-marginal automobiles. Such a requirement, which would ensure growing benefits from traffic, might well entail an optimal flow with very few private automobiles.

Be that as it may, it is only *after* this optimal flow is established that one may proceed correctly to estimate the returns to investment in road-widening, freeways and other traffic-accommodating projects. A traffic flow that has not been corrected implies that marginal congestion costs exceed marginal benefit for some part of the existing traffic flow. Total congestion costs incurred being, then, so much greater than the optimally determined congestion costs, the saving by traffic investment will appear correspondingly greater. It is possible, therefore, that an initial optimal traffic flow might reveal no economic case for traffic investment, whereas failure to establish this optimal flow would allow traffic to pile up congestion costs and would therefore enable investment to appear profitable in effect by reducing excess traffic costs that were not warranted in the first place.

Similar remarks apply to our second illustration. If as a consequence of rail closure congestion occurs on the road connecting the suburb to the city, the establishment of an optimal flow of motorized traffic must precede any estimate of the benefits of road investment. More important, the rationale of the proposed rail closure itself should be scrutinized before this requirement. A fall in the number of fare-paying passengers below some critical number n is generally irrelevant in this connection. The line should be kept running for the time being, if, at any number of passengers for which price is equal to marginal operating costs, total benefit exceeds total operating costs.[1] Benefits may be reckoned as the sum of three items: (*a*) the fares that could be collected of all those willing to pay the marginal cost price (as determined by the existing demand schedule) plus the consumer's surplus of every such individual; (*b*) the insurance value of the railway service to those who do not anticipate any particular railway journeys; and (*c*) the sum total of any (additional) congestion costs that would be inflicted on all motorists having to use the suburb-to-city road after the railway closure.[2] It would not be surprising if many of the railway services closed

[1] Largely the earnings of *necessary* personnel, fuel and maintenance charges.

[2] To be more exact (*c*) should be included in so far as this contingent addition to congestion has not been anticipated. If it were wholly anticipated, it would

or due for closure could prove economic viability by meeting these conditions. At all events, closing a railway service that, on this criterion, ought not to be closed, entails a misallocation of shiftable resources currently being used by the railway. Having misallocated resources by closing down the railway service, investment in roads that would otherwise (if the railway service were available) be clearly seen as wasteful might well appear profitable.

IV

We have confined ourselves in this note to diseconomies that are internal to private motoring, i.e. to the mutual congestion costs of motorized traffic, following the popular custom of relegating to a parenthetical remark the unmeasurable, though probably much more important, effects on the physical environment. The private car carries along with it, however, a much neglected disamenity-potential through its being the chief agent of rapid urban sprawl and ribbon building. As 'developers' set up estates farther and yet farther from city centres, in the assurance that wherever they site their buildings families with private cars will be prepared to make the longer journey in order to live in country areas, the advantages of those families already settled in these areas are diminished.[1]

Even if we restrict the analysis to a given area, say the city and its dormitory areas, the continual visual disturbance, the pollution of the air by exhaust fumes, the incessant engine noise and vibration generated by any n travellers using private transport is very many times that generated by the same number using public transport instead, in particular if public transport were electrically powered. Hence, although an optimal flow of traffic calculated with respect only to mutual traffic frustration already favours public transport at the expense of private

---

have raised the consumers' surpluses of existing, and potential, railway users, and would have raised the value of the railway to motorists who make no regular use of the railway.

[1]Again, however, if some institutional mechanism could be established whereby each additional home-buyer (who adds to the existing number in or near the area and so contributes to its transformation into a suburb) were obliged to compensate existing householders for the loss of amenity endured by his settling there, the criterion for an improvement could be met. Such diseconomies would then be automatically corrected and urban sprawl be subject to a built-in check.

transport (comparing this optimal flow with the usual free-for-all that makes road investment appear so profitable), an optimal flow that also takes into consideration these other environment-damaging consequences – no less relevant or significant for being statistically elusive – would further reduce the warrantable flow of private traffic. If the number of private car journeys consistent with this more comprehensive measure of the optimal flow were believed to be few, the costs involved in their regulation might well suggest the prohibition within a given area of all private traffic as the most economic solution – allowing, perhaps, for a given number of private taxis within the area for emergency purposes.

It may well happen that, contrary to our initial assumption, the existing public transport was inadequate in the first place with respect to coverage, speed and frequency. However, an analysis that yields an optimal solution requiring the provision of an efficient public transport service does not depend upon the chronological sequence posited for its validity.[1]

---

[1] In general, if each vehicle differed in size and other relevant characteristics, and if the value attached by the occupants of each vehicle to travelling the distance in question differed for any i^{th} journey, we should determine the optimal traffic flow and its composition by maximizing the social surplus. This is got by ranking the individual journeys by the excess of CS over the marginal congestion cost until the excess is zero. In the absence of welfare effects on the CS measure, which would be brought into operation by compensatory payments, the optimal flow and composition of the traffic is uniquely determined. For any flow having a social surplus smaller than this maximum indicates a potential improvement. Thus some journey(s) currently excluded by the composition of the existing traffic could replace some journey(s) currently included, and thereby increase the social surplus. The additional gain from such exchange operations could, of course, be distributed among the participants as to make each of them better off.